simply
palmistry

simply

palmistry

SASHA FENTON

A Sterling / Zambezi Book
Sterling Publishing Co., Inc.
New York

Library of Congress Cataloging-in-Publication Data Available

2   4   6   8   10   9   7   5   3

Published in 2005 by Sterling Publishing Co., Inc.
387 Park Avenue South, New York, NY 10016
Copyright © 2005 Sasha Fenton
Illustrations Copyright © 2005 Hannah Firmin
Palm Illustrations Copyright © 2003 Malcolm Wright
Published and distributed in the UK solely by Zambezi Publishing Limited
P.O. Box 221, Plymouth, Devon PL2 2YJ
Distributed in Canada by Sterling Publishing
c/o Canadian Manda Group, 165 Dufferin Street
Toronto, Ontario, Canada M6K 3H6
Distributed in Australia by Capricorn Link (Australia) Pty. Ltd.
P.O. Box 704, Windsor, NSW 2756, Australia

For information about custom editions, special sales, premium and
corporate purchases, please contact Sterling Special Sales
Department at 800-805-5489 or specialsales@sterlingpub.com.

Manufactured in China

Sterling ISBN 13: 978-1-4027-2275-2
ISBN 10: 1-4027-2275-3

contents

Introduction *6*

1 Check Out That Man! *9*

2 Who's That Girl? *19*

3 The Map of the Hand *27*

4 The Fingers *41*

5 The Phalanges *55*

6 The Major Lines *63*

7 The Minor Lines *93*

8 Love and Relationships *105*

9 Marks *117*

10 Health on the Hands *125*

11 Back to the Beginning *133*

12 How to Make Handprints *143*

Index *157*

introduction

Hand reading is easy. In this book, I show how easy it is to read hands for fun and pleasure. I even show how to size someone up without them knowing that you are doing it. In fact, I start this book by setting a scene where a woman, then a man, who are out on the town spot someone attractive and want to know a little more about them. I show how they can do this just by looking casually at their hands. Use this book and practice on your friends to see how close you can get to their characters, objectives, and goals. A little palmistry knowledge can give you a lot of fun, and it never fails to impress.

After the fun section, I cover the basics of hand reading, including the lines, mounts, fingers, and thumb—all the other components that relate to the subject. I show how to judge someone's character and long-term destiny. I tend to use the masculine "he" and "him" in books such as this because it makes them easier to read. Naturally, everything in my book relates to both sexes and every type of person. At the end of the book, I return to the theme of checking out a new acquaintance, this time to judge how you would get along together.

This book will not turn you into a professional hand reader overnight. That takes years of practice and tons of knowledge, but if it encourages you to seek more insight into the subject of hand reading, you can always move on to the heavy stuff later.

So, for now, take the easy route to developing your knowledge and your social skills with this simple *Simply* book.

Good luck.

1

CHECK OUT THAT MAN!

You and your friends are enjoying a night out on the town and you spot an interesting-looking guy, but how can you judge on first acquaintance whether he is a lover or a loser? Well, there is a way that you can give him the once-over without him even knowing what you are up to. You can check out his hands even at a distance of a few feet. Now, we don't all want the same thing from our men, so what you see might suit you but not your friend—and what you see may make you feel that this man has the potential to be Mr. Right, or perhaps just Mr. Right For the Time Being . . .

HAND SIZE

Start by observing the size of his hands, bearing in mind the size of the man as a whole. Do they seem to fit him properly? Are they too large or too small for his frame? A discrepancy here means an imbalance in his nature, because his hands should have some connection to the rest of his body.

His Hands Are Small

A man with small hands is a busy man and he works hard. He may be a hot number at sales and marketing or he may be a clever moneymaker. If his hands are rather hard and firm-looking, he will be able to read a balance sheet at a glance, and he can make a deal. If they are soft, his aptitude will be for sales, marketing, and persuasion. Either way, this man is quite likely to commit to a relationship, because he has committed himself to working for a living. Whether he is available, or even interested, in a long-term relationship remains to be seen.

Try to judge whether the hands are rounded, as this denotes sociability and a desire for variety in life. This man makes friends easily and has a sense of the ridiculous, but he easily becomes bored, so you must stay on your toes to keep him interested.

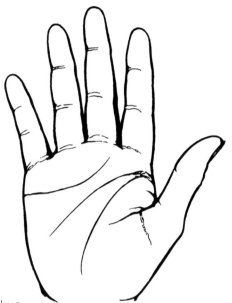

Rounded hands

This guy wants a base, a home, and possibly a family, but he loves to move about in search of opportunities and as part of his job. He probably enjoys traveling, so even if he has not reached that moment in life when he feels the need to settle down, he could be up for an exotic vacation in good company—your company, perhaps. This guy is quick to think, act, move, and make up his mind, but he can change it just as quickly. If you do travel with this man, be prepared to move around. He can lie on a beach only until he has finished reading his book or listening to the ball game on his radio. Once that is over, he will be ready to look around and see what the place has to offer. After forty-eight hours, he may be ready to go home, get back to work, or find another holiday location. If he disappears for a few hours, he might even have found a new partner! It may be just as well to pack some books yourself, because you could spend the next few days alone—or with someone else.

Small, Less Developed Hands

If his hand looks somewhat undeveloped, with stubby fingers and few lines showing on it, he may be very pedestrian and have elementary hands. He is unwilling to try anything new or to be too adventurous, because he prefers a regular job and a well-ordered life. Unfortunately, he may also have a short fuse due to his inability to express himself.

If his hands are shapelier than the elementary kind, and if they look rather firm, he is the hard-working type who could well be on the road to success. If his cell phone rings constantly, he is probably keeping in touch with his office—or a string of partners!

Elementary hands

When it comes to lovemaking, he knows what to do—after all, he has had plenty of partners to practice on. Do not expect him to spend day after day in languorous lovemaking, though, because he gets bored with everything—even his own pleasures. He soon feels the need to get up, look for something to eat, check out the progress of his sports team, phone the office, and even send a text message to his mother—or perhaps his ex-partner!

He is quick on the uptake, so he will grasp what you tell him in an instant, but he will not want to listen to long stories or hear about your "feelings." His downside is a quick temper and a sharp, sarcastic tongue. When he suddenly turns on you, you will wonder whether all those lovely things he said to you yesterday (this morning, half an hour ago) were true, or whether he really thinks so little of you. However, the sun soon comes out again and you forgive him. He is all sweetness and light, until the next bout of "aggressive mouth syndrome."

Depending on your nature (and your hand shape), you might put up with this in the hope that he will improve, or put up with it until you can drop him. If his hands are small, rounded, and soft, don't expect him to come around and put up shelves for you. He is not into physical activities—indeed he may not be interested in any kind of activity! However, he does have a quick and able brain when he chooses to use it.

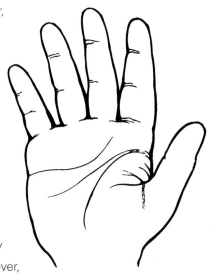

Small, soft hands

If his hands are small and square, this man not only does things at speed, but he also has a practical and sensible turn of mind.

His Hands Are Large

This is an altogether slower type of man. He is thoughtful and he appears to be really interested in what you have to say. If his hands are square, he has a practical nature, so if your apartment happens to need some plumbing or electrical work, he is worth cultivating! This man can cope with details, so you could even persuade him to fix your hair braids while he is sorting out your scrambled telephone wires.

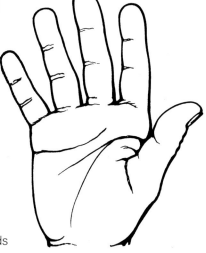

Square hands

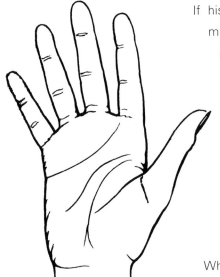

Long, delicate hands

If his hands are slim and fine, he is artistic or musical, and at times he will be completely absorbed in his own interests. While this man is interesting to be with on a short-term basis, he may be less ready to settle for a mundane family life. You may end up sitting on the sidelines while he goes out on a Friday night, even though this makes you feel vaguely like a groupie. An artist will always have some etching that he is ready to show you . . .

When it comes to lovemaking, it is worth getting in some food and drink supplies. He will snuggle down in your apartment for the duration, so make a checklist that includes cherries, grapes, a bottle of wine, and the name of a decent Chinese takeout. He is a good conversationalist, so you can expect to hear all about his work (he doesn't like it much), his ex-partner (who didn't understand him), and his successes in the backgammon competition. When you have had enough of this, ensure that you have some decent CDs to play. He will appreciate them and you can nod off for a while.

If his hands are medium to large, and they look knobbly or knotted, especially around the knuckles, he will take his time over things.

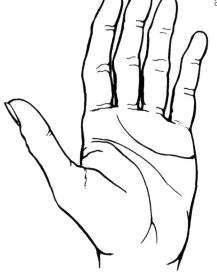

Knotty or
knobby hands

He is a thinker. While he can move quickly when necessary, he doesn't like to make arrangements without knowing what he is letting himself in for.

Regardless of the size of a man's hand, here are a few other things to watch for. If you appreciate a sensitive man who will really hear what you say, look at the backs of his hands. If the veins show through or if they are prominent, this man is Mr. Sensitivity. The problem is that it is easy to hurt him. He may have learned to protect himself by behaving coldly or by finding ways to trip others up and make them feel like fools. If the veins do not show, he is less into his own feelings and less easy to upset. This makes him reliable, but he may not be too interested in hearing about your feelings.

Look at the edge of his hand, which palmists call the "percussion." When the percussion is thick and meaty, and especially if it has an outward bulge, very little will shock him. He may lose his temper easily, and he could even become violent or upset if he has too much to drink.

Thick "percussion" edge

If you want a man to keep you in the style to which you are (or would like to be) accustomed, you must look for one with firm hands, as this is the sign of a hard worker. Soft hands spell self-indulgence, while bony hands that look a bit like a chicken's feet are too sensitive to cope with sustained effort or stress.

RIGHT–HANDED OR LEFT–HANDED?

Is he right- or left-handed? This isn't so easy to spot at a glance, but watch to see whether he holds his glass in his right or left hand when drinking. If he is eating, see how he uses his fork. If he uses his hands while talking, notice the hand he uses most. If you get a chance to talk to him, ask him to write something down, as even quite ambidextrous people tend to use their dominant hand when writing.

Right-handed people are in the majority; so if you like an ordinary type of guy whose head isn't full of artistic waffle, this is the man for you. However, you may find an artistic, creative, left-field type of person more interesting, so don't throw out the left-hander with the bathwater. The logical, numeric, left side of the brain rules right-handed people, so these folk frequently have ordinary jobs and lives, although they may balance this with an unusual hobby. The spatial, pictorial, right side of the brain rules left-handed people, so they prefer careers such as hypnotherapy, art, music, or any creative field. They may have a practical job as a fallback position, but their real love might be playing unusual musical instruments, collecting ancient Greek pots—or psychology.

2

WHO'S THAT GIRL?

Those of us who write and publish books on fortune-telling know that most of our readers are female, but many of us live with men or have men around. A man will take a peep at our books whenever there is something marginally less interesting to watch on the television than a bunch of guys tossing and kicking a leather-covered pig's bladder around a field. Therefore, for the men (or for those who keep an eye on you), here is the secret to finding perfect love—or something . . .

Lord Byron once said something to the effect that men have many interests, but women's main (or only) interest is love. That may have been the case in eighteen hundred and something, and it still holds true today. This said, most men do reach a "moment." By this I mean that a man who has been perfectly happy to live with his parents, run around with his friends, date casually, or focus on his work suddenly reaches a "moment" when the idea of a wife and family appeals to him. Women never have to reach this "moment" because we are in it all our lives. Women are always at the stage of hoping to meet someone, hoping to lose the one they have, trying to get over the loss of someone—or hoping to meet someone new . . . if you see what I mean!

A man may reach one of these "moments" at any time . . . perhaps when he is sitting around in a retirement home. However, whether you are at your "moment" or just looking for someone to while away some of your spare time, the following should help you to find what you want and avoid traps that await the unwary.

LARGE OR SMALL HANDS

The rules here are much the same as in the previous section. In short, a woman with small hands rushes around and gets things done, but she may move on to something (or someone) else quite quickly. A woman who has large hands is slower, but she is capable of fine and detailed work. She also stays put through thick and thin. Speaking of thick and thin, a woman with small hands is more likely to put on weight as she gets older. Some women with larger hands can gain weight, but they are less likely to do so.

WHAT WILL SHE SETTLE FOR?

The ulna side of the hand (the side opposite to the thumb) is associated with home, family, relationships, and friends. So if you want a woman who is the old-fashioned kind, who will make chicken soup and run the home well, look for one whose hands are fully developed on the ulna side. The ring and little fingers should be fairly long and the edge of her hand firm.

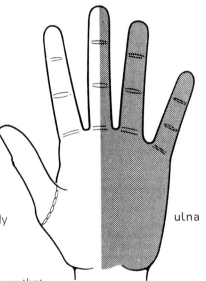

ulna

The ulna side of the hand

A firm hand belongs to a hard worker who will ensure that her home runs smoothly and that there is enough money coming in to cover the bills, but this woman will also expect some input from you. If you choose a sweet girl with soft, squashy hands, she may be very appealing in the short term, but in time, you might get sick of providing everything for the two of you—especially when she tells you that it is still not enough.

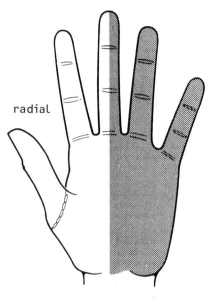

radial

The radial (thumb) side of the hand is more interested in what is going on in the world. A developed radial side belongs to a woman who is likely to have a career or outside interests. She will not be easy to dominate and control, especially if the index finger and thumb look firm and strong.

There is something unappealing about a woman with bony hands. She seems to want more than any man (or anyone) can give. Her hands may be medium-sized and angular, which means that she wants to live in a certain style and certainly to travel in comfort. If her hands and fingernails resemble claws, her materialism can reach sky-high.

The radial side of the hand

Look at the shape of her hands and of her fingertips. Squareness always indicates practicality and common sense. Square or spatulate fingertips show a good mind and an aptitude for playing classical music or for figure work, embroidery, or something else that involves details. This may or may not interest you greatly, but it is always useful for a girl to have a nice hobby.

Clawlike hands

It doesn't take much brainpower to see that long, slim hands are artistic and sensitive. Look at the back of them and see whether the veins show, as this will tell you whether she will be sensitive to your feelings. If the veins are buried beneath fat or a thick skin, you might as well give up the idea of expressing your feelings—she just won't understand you. Rounded hands are sociable, friendly, accommodating, fond of vacations, changes of scene, and life itself. However, this woman can get bored quite easily, so you will have to work hard to keep her interest.

PASSION

Most men are interested in sex—at least all those who have a fully developed little finger are! So how do you find a passionate woman? The answer is not easy, because the obvious seat of passion is the famous "mount of Venus" on the hand.

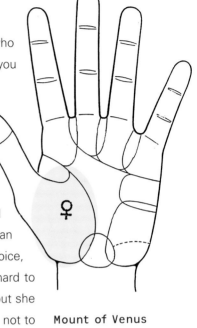

If this area of the hand is large, it shows passion for something. While this can be for sex, it can also be for material things such as goods, money, and essentials such as Manolo shoes. In one way, a woman with a well-developed Venus mount can be a good choice, because she lives life to the fullest. She will work hard to make a nice home and to have money in the bank, but she will also be a loving companion. However, be careful not to judge this mount by its height alone, because a wide mount of Venus is better than a full one. Fullness here suggests self-indulgence and selfishness, and if the mount is high and hard-packed, it denotes a demanding and selfish nature—albeit a sexy one.

Mount of Venus

A cramped Venus mount belongs to someone who will settle for a lot less and who makes few demands, but this woman has a fertile mind and lives "in her head." She may prefer to stay at home and live a quiet life. This could suit some men admirably, but if you want a woman who will join you on a nice hike up Mount Kilimanjaro or a holiday in a longhouse in Borneo, you will be disappointed.

A sexually imaginative woman will also have a full Luna mount, and possibly a strange pattern in the skin prints.

I have known women with this mount who take an interest in Tantric sex and other interesting forms of activity. If you are into experimentation, this is the girl for you, but if you are a nervous Capricorn who prefers not to encounter too many surprises in the bedroom, perhaps you should avoid this type.

Sensible men prefer an intelligent partner, so look for long first phalanges on the fingers for at least some indication of brainpower.

The first phalange on a finger

Short first phalanges belong to someone who thinks less but possibly achieves more.

MONEY AND SHOPPING

Try this little experiment. Listen to a group of men talking. It doesn't matter where you are at the time—at work, in a social setting, in a line at the movies, or lining up to get into the gym. Most men talk about money. They discuss the house, business, car, tools, sports equipment, camping equipment, or mountain bike that they have bought, are considering buying, that their friend has bought or that they would love to buy. Female shopping is frequent and small in comparison to that of men, who think, agonize, talk, and dream about what they want for months—and then, when the moon is in a funny phase, rush out and buy it.

All women love shopping—apart from the weekly run around the supermarket, of course. However, if you need to be sure that your lady will come back from the shops with more or less what she said she was going out to buy, choose one whose thumbs are straight. If the thumbs turn back, she will go out for one thing and come back with something quite different—and much more expensive!

I have straight thumbs, so I may deviate from my intention to buy cabbage and come back with a pair of socks. My first husband, Tony Fenton, had very flexible thumb tips. He once went out for a newspaper and bought a house! It was a nice house, though, and we lived in it for thirty-two years.

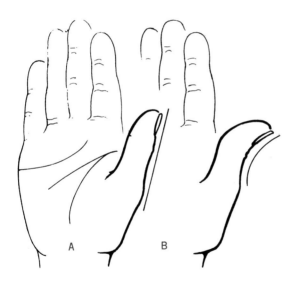

Hand A has a stiff thumb and hand B
has a flexible thumb

3

THE MAP OF THE HAND

APOLLO	artistry, creativity, the family, leisure activities
LUNA	the imagination, travel and restlessness, creativity, the unconscious mind
MERCURY	communication, work, elementary education, interests, literacy and numeracy, dexterity, health, sexuality
VENUS	luxury, possessions, ownership, love of beauty, passion, friendship, love, affection
MARS	aggression and assertiveness, courage, enthusiasm, energy, military matters
JUPITER	belief, leadership qualities, ego, teaching ability
SATURN	science, study, practical matters, hard work, structure, financial security, old age
URANUS	not yet used in palmistry
NEPTUNE	imagination, psychic perception; the bridge between the conscious and unconscious, and a bridge between the spiritual and the practical world
PLUTO	travel, escapism, restlessness, boredom with ordinary life

So now let us consider a few details. The first thing to grasp is that each area of the hand applies to a different area of life. Looking at a hand is rather like reading the kind of map that surveys the landscape and shows the features of its terrain. Each part of the hand is associated with a particular attribute or interest in the subject's life.

The Indo-European palmistry that we use has links to the planets in astrology, but there are subtle differences between a palmist's views of the planetary connections and those of astrologers. As an astrologer and a palmist, I feel that the palmist's view of the planetary meanings harks back to the early days of astrology. Modern Western astrology has drifted away somewhat from these basics. Here is a brief introduction to the way palmists view the planets and their associated areas of the hand.

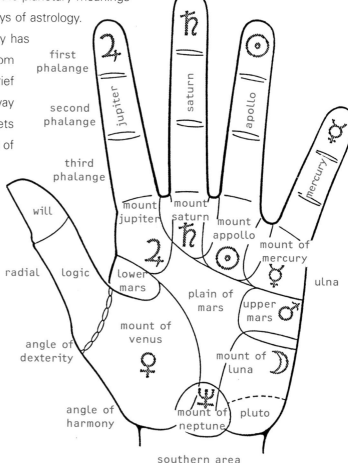

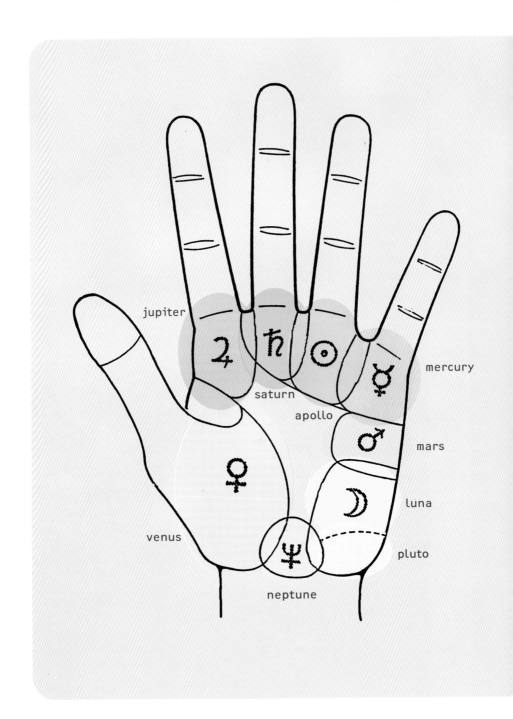

THE MOUNTS

Palmists call the areas on the palm of a hand mounts, despite the fact that some look more like valleys. In this chapter and elsewhere in this book, I occasionally refer to mounts being larger, smaller, higher, lower, narrower, or wider than normal. I am aware that this is hard for a beginner to judge, so I suggest that you line up a half dozen of your friends and see how their hands vary. You will see that most of the mounts are similar on most of their hands, but one person among them will have a mount that is higher and larger than the others and vice versa. This will give you some idea of the differences that you can see in a bunch of hands.

The Mount of Jupiter

This mount lies directly below the Jupiter finger. It relates to the ego, self-belief, and the chances of success. It also concerns honesty, wisdom, and idealism. It is good to have a moderate mount of Jupiter, but a high one suggests that the person is so self-centered that he cannot see the needs of others. A high mount signifies an overinflated ego, while a flat one shows a lack of confidence but also a capacity for hard work. If a cross appears on this mount, it signifies marriage to someone who has money.

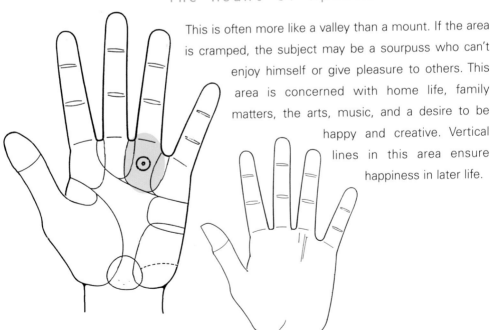

The Mount of Saturn

The Saturn area rarely forms a mount. If there is a fleshy area between the Saturn and Apollo fingers, the individual has a certain sense of style and the ability to work hard at something creative. If this area is shallow—that is, if there is very little space between the base of the fingers and the heart line—the subject may be materialistic and unable to show affection or give love. This area is mainly concerned with practical matters such as security, keeping a roof over one's head, money, resources, and to some extent, career and business matters. Lines that run vertically up this mount demonstrate a desire for security and perhaps concerns about finances later in life.

The Mount of Apollo

This is often more like a valley than a mount. If the area is cramped, the subject may be a sourpuss who can't enjoy himself or give pleasure to others. This area is concerned with home life, family matters, the arts, music, and a desire to be happy and creative. Vertical lines in this area ensure happiness in later life.

Happiness later in life

The Mount of Mercury

If the Mercury mount is substantial and full, the person will be intelligent and will have a talent for communication and for listening to others. He may work with machinery or he may teach. A cross here shows technical ability, such as working with computers and other equipment. It can also mean playing an instrument or being a clever engineer.

This area is also concerned with health and healing, so marks here indicate a talent for healing. There may be three diagonal lines running vertically up this mount, signifying an ability to provide healing, either though conventional medicine or as a spiritual healer.

The mark of a healer

The Mount of Venus

The mount of Venus relates to desire, passion, and the feel-good factor. Tradition tells us that a person with a large and prominent mount of Venus is sexy, but he is certainly passionate. He may be passionate about collecting art, music, the theater, his home and family, gourmet food, travel, keeping horses, or something else entirely. The passion is less likely to be for a cause or political or spiritual belief and more likely to be for something personal.

If this mount is full and high, the subject craves beauty, possessions, and luxury and may be possessive. A well-developed Venus endows an individual with energy and determination and is often an indicator of potential or actual worldly success. If this mount is too large or too high, it shows self-indulgence, greed, laziness, selfishness, too much sexuality, and a jealous or bullying nature. If this person has the right combination of characteistics, he will be highly successful, as the desire to have what he wants will spur him on. However, laziness and a love of luxury may be his downfall.

A flat mount of Venus still endows energy as long as the area is large. This subject is bighearted and generous. Large Venus mounts, whether high or low, usually tell us that this person will make money—mainly because he cannot stand the thought of having to budget or do without the things he likes, but also because he doesn't wish to depend upon others.

If the mount is cramped, the subject may be happy to get along with few possessions in favor of the freedom to be himself. He may be miserly and remote with a preference for a lonely, Spartan lifestyle. He may still be sociable and even sexual, but he is not interested in living with others or cluttering up his life with many possessions. He will not make an all-out effort to succeed in a career and may well prefer an easy life or a small, quiet world of his own making.

A creative person with a large Venus mount will make objects that are attractive and useful. The person with a smaller mount is analytical, precise, logical, wordy, and left-brain oriented.

Lines and creases on the mount of Venus indicate difficulties in making or keeping money. Lines on the edge of the hand coming into the Venus area denote friendships, membership in groups, clubs, or committees, and social life.

The Mount of Luna

The mount of Luna is associated with travel—traditionally on or over the sea. It is also concerned with imagination and creativity, and to some extent, psychic talents.

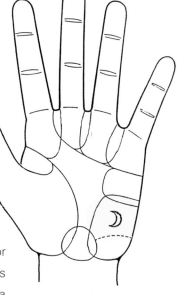

The ancients considered the Moon restless because it traveled quickly across the sky, disappeared altogether for a while, and then appeared again during the course of each month. A large and prominent Luna signifies a restless person who enjoys travel and adventure. He may choose a career that takes him from place to place, or he will travel for fun. Whether high or flat, a sizable Luna shows a love for the countryside and the sea. A prominent Luna indicates creativity and a powerful imagination. Obviously, if this area is flat and cramped, the subject does not enjoy travel and he may not have much imagination either.

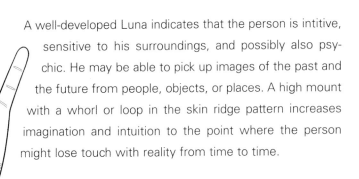

A well-developed Luna indicates that the person is intitive, sensitive to his surroundings, and possibly also psychic. He may be able to pick up images of the past and the future from people, objects, or places. A high mount with a whorl or loop in the skin ridge pattern increases imagination and intuition to the point where the person might lose touch with reality from time to time.

The Mount of Pluto

Right at the bottom of this mount is a bone just above the place where the hand joins the wrist. Modern palmists now call this area the mount of Pluto. I think they have just given it this name for the sake of convenience, because it has nothing to do with the Pluto with which astrologers are familiar.

When the Pluto mount is high and wide, the person is very restless; he is a real traveler. He gets bored quickly unless he is on the move. If the mount is scarcely visible or curves sharply inward at the percussion edge, he may enjoy the occasional week's holiday, but he really prefers to be at home.

Mounts of Venus, Luna, and Pluto The easiest way to think about these mounts is to consider that Venus loves people and things that can be experienced with the five senses. Luna and Pluto represent a love of travel and those things that are beyond the physical senses.

The Mounts of Mars

Now things get a little complicated. The whole of the central area of the hand is devoted to Mars, but it is subdivided into upper Mars, lower Mars, and the plain of Mars.

Upper Mars Upper Mars is located at the percussion edge of the hand, and this relates to fighting ability and reactions such as anger and belligerence. It is hard to shock the individual on which this area is high or if there is thickness throughout the hand. He may fight with words or with his fists, but he will not put up with anything that he doesn't like. This person may choose to serve in the armed forces, the police, or the fire department or as an emergency medic. He enjoys being where the action is. However, if the upper Mars area bows outward at the edge, he has creative talent and he may work with his mind and hands in a creative manner. He may also be unreliable or even crooked, because what he wants is important to him and he doesn't much care how he gets it.

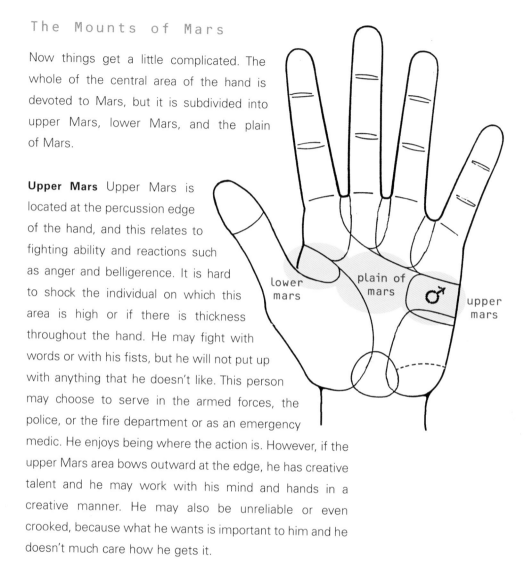

If this area is thin, the subject is nervous. He may have been bullied when he was young, and he never really developed much courage. If he tucks his thumb into his fingers, he is very nervous, frightened, and unsure of himself. This gesture gives him a form of self-comfort and reassurance.

If the edge of the hand is straight rather than bowed, the subject is a good record keeper, proofreader, secretary, or analyst. He can interpret and improve the ideas of others but he may not be creative in his own right.

Lower Mars Lower Mars is often actually higher on the hand than upper Mars. Lower Mars is located on the hand and palm around and below where the thumb opens away from the hand; it is inside the lifeline. Someone with a prominent, large, or "full" lower Mars mount can be counted on to do his duty. As a youngster, he may have been a Scout, a cadet, or something of that kind. He is a good team member, especially if there is serious work to be done, and he would thoroughly enjoy a spell as a military leader.

A flat, indented, or cramped area here belongs to an individual who sees no need to join pressure groups or to get into uniform. He's probably too unconventional and independent to be a good team member.

The plain of Mars is the flat area in the center of the hand. While each mount relates to a specific aspect of life (status, family, life, travel, etc.), the plain of Mars does not. Many lines traverse the area, and a skilled palmist can spot health problems arising from the marks and colored patches that appear in the area.

The Mount of Neptune

Neptune represents a link between the conscious and unconscious mind and also between the spiritual and the material world. Psychics, spiritual mediums, artists, psychologists, dream analysts, creative people, and those who travel a great deal have well-developed Neptune mounts. This links the material world of Venus with the imaginative or psychic world of Luna. It also links the conscious and unconscious mind.

ANGLES

The joint where the thumb meets the hand is the angle of dexterity. If it is reasonably well developed, the person has a certain gracefulness, he rarely drops anything, and he is good with his hands. He also has a sense of timing. This is useful if he enjoys music—including hip-hop and rap—dancing, and sports. This man has the kind of timing that makes him good at telling jokes. He has an instinctive feel for the right time to speak or to clam up.

The angle at the base of the hand on the thumb side is called the angle of harmony. If it is sharply angular and has a marked "corner," the subject has a profound interest in music, and may very well be a singer or musician.

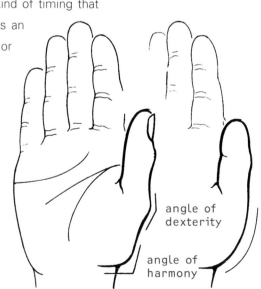

angle of
dexterity

angle of
harmony

4

THE FINGERS

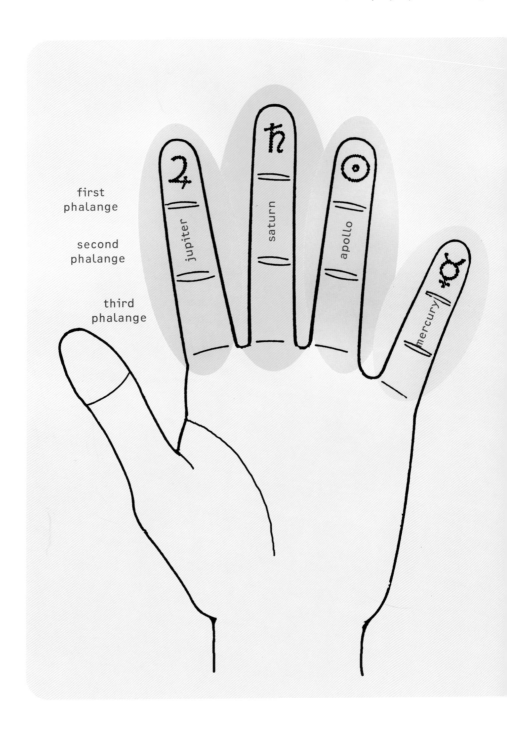

first
phalange

second
phalange

third
phalange

Earlier, we had fun with the idea of examining hands without someone realizing that we are doing so. To some extent, we can also do this with the fingers, although, obviously, we cannot see everything on them from a distance.

Fingers come in all shapes and sizes, with a large variety of tips and fingernails. They can curve in different directions and their relative length can be deceptive.

SETTING

It is actually worth using a ruler when assessing the true length of one finger against another, as the way that they are set onto the palm can vary. Some are set in a straight line at the base, while others curve down from the index to the little finger and yet others are set in an arc.

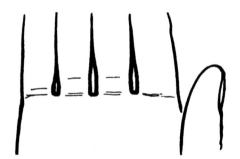

Finger settings can vary

When fingers are in line, the top of the palm is obviously also straight, suggesting practicality.

A creative or sensitive person has fingers arrayed an arc. This also indicates mental dexterity. Musical and artistic people sometimes have fingers set on a slope running downward from the index finger to the little finger.

Fingers can be long, short, fat, thin, smooth, or knotty. Short fingers denote physical energy while longer ones suggest a dreamy personality. Knotty knuckles belong to a deep thinker who does everything at his own pace and who hates to be rushed, while smooth fingers signify less thought but more speed and action.

INCLINATION

The outlines in this illustration are a dramatic demonstration of the way that the fingers bend toward or away from each other.

Jupiter Bends Outward

A Jupiter finger that pulls away and bends outward belongs to someone who likes to think and act independently. If this feature is strong, it signifies a truly awkward personality who will not listen to others.

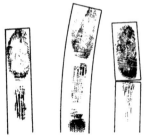

Inclining fingers

If the Jupiter finger inclines toward the Saturn finger, other people have too much influence over the subject. He listens to them because he is unsure of himself and he needs their approval. This may make it easy for people who have stronger characters to dominate him or push him into doing the things they want rather than what is best for him.

Saturn and Apollo Apart

A V-shaped gap between the Saturn and Apollo fingers belongs to an independent person who might be a rebel. He has strong opinions and a critical tongue.

If the Saturn and Apollo fingers cling together, the individual needs a job that gives him fulfillment and happiness. He needs to work (Saturn) at something that he enjoys and that has a creative slant (Apollo). He tries to maintain a balance among family life, career, and his belief system, and often feels guilty when he fails.

Mercury Pulls Away

When the Mercury finger pulls away from the Apollo finger, the individual doesn't rush into commitment in relationships and partnerships, but he is also slow to leave them. Bends and kinks in this finger denote obstinacy.

RELAXED OR TIGHTLY CURLED FINGERS

When someone is relaxed and content with life, his fingers relax, but when he is uptight, they curl into a fist. When he is frightened, he tucks his thumb into his fist.

THE LONG AND THE SHORT

Fingers are hard to assess when looked at singly. Try looking at the back of the hand, as this makes it easier.

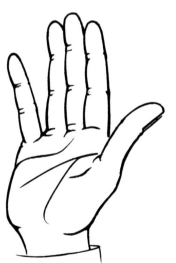

Saturn and Apollo
fingers close together

Mercury finger
pulling away

THE FOUR FINGERS

The Jupiter Finger

A long Jupiter finger signifies self-belief, a strong ego, and self-motivation. It also shows independence, leadership, and enough courage to give speeches or fight for a cause. This subject will not compromise or bend to the will of others, and he may be argumentative. He works with others, but he may end up leading them. If the finger is fat, he might be a bully.

When this finger is short, others can persuade or coerce him. He will try to fit in with the views of those around him. Alternatively, he may quietly go his own way, working alone and achieving success without controlling or organizing others. When the Mercury finger bends toward the Saturn one, the person can be a good salesperson, but he needs to handle a product that he can believe in.

The Saturn Finger

If the Saturn finger is long, the individual may work in a highly technical field where he can put his intellect to good use. He does not spend money freely, especially if he has square fingertips and nails. He may be serious, dour, or tightfisted. Though he may not be a hard worker, he will certainly have a fine mind. He will spend a good deal of time studying or thinking, and he could be a good teacher. If the Jupiter finger is also long, he will have strong religious or philosophical views.

When the Saturn finger is short, the subject has a talent for acting or for other types of entertainment and performing. He may be a gambler, a con artist, a waster, or someone who simply uses his acting talents as an honest and successful salesperson.

The Apollo Finger

A long Apollo finger signifies sensitivity and feelings. The person may also be sexy and loving, as his needs and emotions are close to the surface. He is creative, artistic, and musical, and he may be a good dancer. Love, family life, and a peaceful, happy home are important to him. A short Apollo finger suggests that these finer and more enjoyable aspects of life are less important than other matters.

The Mercury Finger

It is hard to measure the Mercury finger correctly, as it is often low-set. Try using a piece of string to check its length against that of the Jupiter finger. If the Mercury finger is the same length as the Jupiter finger, it is average or long.

A long Mercury finger belongs to a good communicator. This subject makes friends easily. He will find and keep lovers due to his ability to talk, listen, and

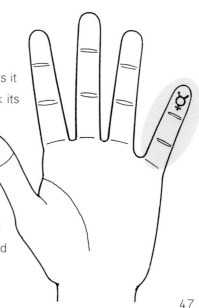

sympathize. This person can cope with machines, equipment, and logical thinking. A short Mercury finger means that the subject finds it hard to express himself. This may cause problems when he tries to communicate clearly with others and also in matters of love and sex. Mentally handicapped people tend to have short and oddly shaped Mercury fingers.

When this finger bends outward, the subject is charming. An inward bend denotes an argumentative or difficult personality. Both bends can suggest obstinacy. If the Mercury finger hooks—rather like the "polite" way of holding a teacup—the person may be extremely stubborn.

If the two upper phalanges are narrower than the base phalange, the person needs affection, cuddles, and sex as a component part of his life.

FINGERTIPS

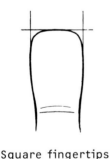

Square fingertips

As with everything else in palmistry, square shapes indicate practicality, persistence, and a tough-minded attitude. When the fingers are thin, the individual has an aptitude for figure work. If you are looking for a good bookkeeper, check the base of the Mercury finger. Little creases at the base of this finger suggest an aptitude for statistical analysis and mathematics.

Look at the fingernails and check whether the tips or bases of them are also square, as this brings a tendency to see everything in terms of black and white. If there is a discrepancy between the nail and fingertip, two different characteristics are present.

Rounded

Rounded fingertips represent sociability and a need for variety. This subject gets on well with people and can be amusing company. He is generous and kind, but also a little lazy—or perhaps just laid back. The best description for this person is normal!

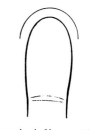

Rounded fingertips

Pointed

Pointed fingertips denote sensitivity and artistic talent, but this person sometimes finds life hard to cope with, especially if the pads of the fingers are also rather flat. He has strong beliefs and he can be hard to influence. He is moral and idealistic.

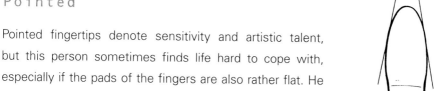

Pointed fingertips

Spatulate

The person with spatulate fingertips is original, artistic, and musical. He believes in himself and he may be quite religious or spiritual. However, he is self-centered and possibly also argumentative. Both the pointed and spatulate finger types can be extremely successful in a creative or artistic endeavor or a bit too dreamy to achieve much in life.

Spatulate fingertips

| Thin fingertips | Thick fingertips | Bulgy fingertip ends |

THICK OR THIN FINGERTIPS

Thicker, heavier fingers imply less brainpower and more energy. These people are practical and they translate ideas into action. Thinner fingers imply intellectual energy but less physical stamina—they may not be able to put their ideas into reality. Droplets or bulgy ends belong to people who have a good eye for design and a strong sense of touch. These people will run their hands over everything because they can almost "see" with the pads on their fingertips.

FINGERNAILS

The following rules for fingernails are similar to those for fingertips. Square nails indicate practicality, while those that are rounded, especially at the base, denote sociability, gen-

| Square nails | Rounded nails | Fan-shaped nails | Wide nails | Narrow nails |

erosity, and friendliness. Narrow nails that show flesh on either side of the hand suggest sensitivity, vulnerability, and a certain amount of caution. Wide nails can talk of a harsh or bullying nature. Fan-shaped nails suggest ambition and a lack of concern for the feelings of others.

FINGERPRINTS

Interestingly, the police use the same terminology for the fingerprints as hand readers do. I sometimes wonder whether any of the fingerprint experts also take an interest in palmistry. The most common patterns are the loop and the whorl, with the loop being the most common print feature. It is not unusual for a person to have loops on all the fingers and both thumbs. A full set of whorls is less common.

The Arch

The arch, or a row of straight lines across a fingertip, rarely shows up on all the fingers. The arch suggests that the person is rather ordinary and that he will work hard throughout life. This also shows that the subject lacks confidence, especially when the arch is on the Jupiter finger or the thumb.

Arch

Tented Arch

The Tented Arch

The tented arch suggests an obsessive, possessive, or fanatical nature, and the finger on which it appears will show where this nature lies. Tented arches appear on the hands of those who fall in love and then hang on with all their might, even when the relationship ends. This is especially so when the tented arch is on Apollo or Mercury. Arches imply some area of self-induced emotional suffering, which can make the person tiresome and self-pitying.

The loop is the most common fingerprint

The Loop

Loops belong to a normal person who likes variety in life and enjoys the company of others. These are either called "ulna loops," when they enter the finger from the outer side of the hand, or "radial loops," when they enter from the thumb side. Ulna loops are common, while radial loops usually occur only on Jupiter and occasionally on Saturn. A radial loop on Jupiter suggests leadership qualities and bossiness. When the radial loop is on the Saturn finger, the subject is clever with his hands.

Whorls are the second most common fingerprint

The Whorl

A whorl represents independence, determination, a go-getting attitude, and selfishness in the area of life defined by the finger in question. However, a whorl on one or two fingers suggests talent in the area related to that finger. Whorls on all ten fingers also signify either a really enterprising and hardworking person or one who was born with a silver spoon in his mouth.

The Peacock's Eye

The peacock's eye fingerprint usually signifies talent. It usually turns up on the Apollo finger, suggesting artistic or musical talent, but possibly also an aptitude for home-making, craftwork, or gardening. If it appears on Mercury, it suggests a gift for acting, public speaking, or writing. This person may be an excellent counselor, nurse, or care assistant. A peacock's eye on the Saturn finger shows talent in a practical field such as technical drawing, carpentry, engineering, building, or civil engineering.

Peacock's Eye

Composite

The composite fingerprint refers to a double loop or double whorl. This person has difficulty in making decisions because both logic and intuition operate at the same time and can sometimes confuse the issue.

5

THE PHALANGES

The bones between the finger and toe joints are called phalanges. There are fourteen phalanges on the hand: three on each finger and two on the thumb.

The top phalanges (these include the fingertips) show how someone thinks. When they are long, the person has an active brain. A fat top phalange shows mental energy, which may be put to some useful purpose, but the energy can also be expended in arguments.

The middle phalanges show how the subject puts his thoughts into action. If they are long, he can act upon his ideas. If they are thin, he may think for a long time and then forget to take action. If they are thick, he will act without thinking.

The lower phalanges show the need for security and comfort. If they are long, the subject will strive to make his life comfortable. If they are fat, he needs both financial and emotional security. Very thick and short lower phalanges may signify a person who eats more than he needs, possibly due to some inborn fear of starvation.

VERTICAL CREASES

Sometimes you will see little vertical creases on the fingers. Unlike fingerprints or skin ridge patterns, these come and go. These creases mean that the person is overtired and probably overdoing things. Horizontal lines indicate that he has more responsibilities than he can really cope with. When life improves, these lines disappear. Horizontal lines on the fingertips suggest a hormone imbalance or some temporary change in the level of hormones.

SOME POINTS TO LOOK FOR

When the fingers are widely spaced at the base and splay out widely, the subject will not hang on to money.

Those with fingertips that turn up tend to work with or for the benefit of the public. They like helping other people, so nurses, social workers, employment agents, and others who help the public often have such fingers.

Fingers that are flexible at the base often indicate someone who likes vacations and a change of scene, as well as a felxible and adaptable personality.

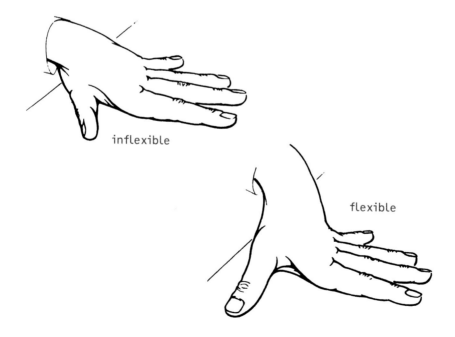

inflexible

flexible

THE THUMB

Many of the rules that apply to the fingers also apply to the thumb. For example, a square tip indicates practicality, a rounded one denotes sociability, a pointed one shows a delicate and idealistic nature, and a spatulate one suggests independence.

A strong-looking thumb denotes determination, strength of purpose, inner toughness, and competitiveness. The person may be a successful athlete, an entrepreneur, a pushy sales clerk or just a strong and powerful personality. A weak-looking thumb signifies a lack of stamina and no interest in competing with others.

If you are looking casually at thumbs while you are out socializing, talk to their owners and judge whether the impression that they give matches up to what you can see on the hand. You will soon notice that the strong-thumbed person appears confident, while the weaker-thumbed person does not. Unfortunately, the one who appears strong may be full of bluster and may lack real inner strength, while the weaker-looking thumb may belong to a quiet person who gets on with things and carries on regardless.

Setting and Inclination

When the thumb is set low, it will open out widely; this shows an open nature. Conversely, a high-set thumb that opens to little more than a 45-degree angle suggests that the person is shy, introverted, and perhaps secretive.

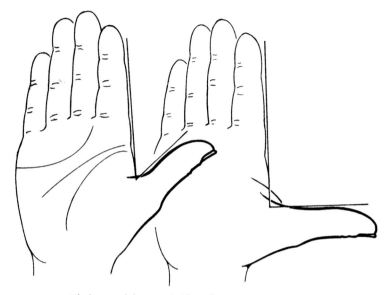

High- and low-set thumbs

A heavy knuckle joint at the base of the thumb shows the need for a physical outlet such as sports, athletics, dancing, or working out in the gym. If the thumb is weaker but the base knuckle still prominent, the subject will be an observer rather than a participant.

A flexible thumb that moves easily at the base belongs to someone who is easily put upon or pushed around. Oddly enough, the muscles and ligaments around the base of the thumb become less flexible over time, suggesting that we are all less likely to put up with bad behavior from others in later life. A stiff thumb tells of someone who digs his heels in and doesn't give way.

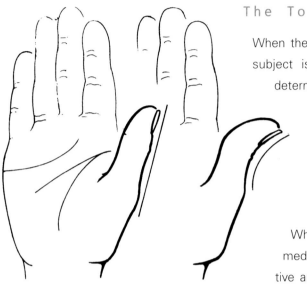

Supple thumbs

The Top Phalange

When the upper phalange dominates, the subject is strong-willed, energetic, and determined. Even if the thumb is not large, a healthy-looking ball joint indicates strength, willpower, and the determination to have one's own way.

When this phalange is rounded and medium-sized, the person is cooperative and pleasant. When it is flat, the subject lacks physical strength, so he uses charm and adaptability to survive. He may bend over backward in his desire for approval.

If the nail side of this phalange is indented or spoon shaped, the subject chisels away until he gets what he wants.

Sometimes the upper part of the thumb curves back. This is the sign of the actor or someone who puts on an act as part of his job. He may be able to manipulate others into believing anything that he says or buying anything that he wants to sell. This subject can be lazy or easily bored, but he is also impulsive. He goes into a shop to buy one thing and comes out with something completely different. If the second phalange is short, he may not think before acting. He can also be selfish and disloyal.

The prints on the thumb also follow the rules of palmistry: A whorl denotes willpower, determination, and independence. A loop denotes a normal, sociable character who enjoys being part of a team. An arch belongs to a hard worker who fears poverty. A tented arch signifies a person who might become fanatical or obsessive. The peacock's eye is a rare formation on the thumb that indicates talent. The double loop or double whorl suggests a combination of intuition, logic, and psychic ability—and indecisiveness.

The Lower Phalange

The second phalange is the phalange of logic. When it is long, the subject thinks before acting, and when it is short, he will act on instinct. A thin phalange with a "waist," or "cinch," suggests a very logical mind and a person who thinks deeply—especially if this phalange is also long. The cinched phalange shows that this sensitive person wants others to like him.

Lines across this phalange suggest fatigue, an unstable home life, or many moves of house or changes of location. If life settles down again, these lines may melt away.

A logical and sensitive nature

6

THE MAJOR LINES

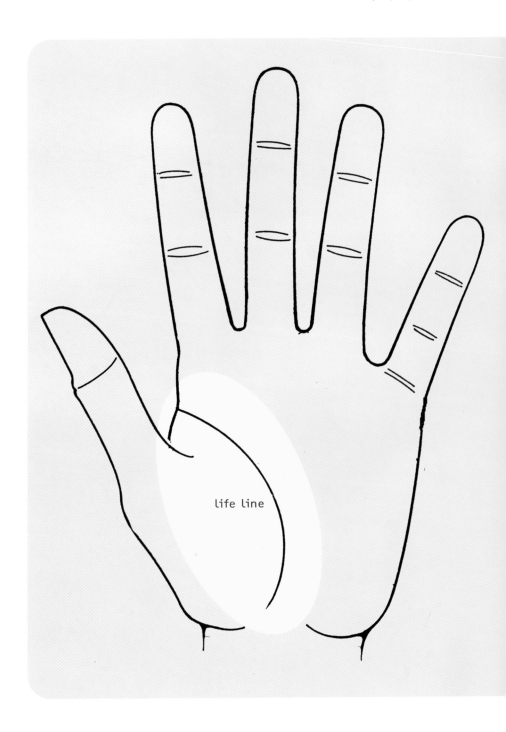

life line

THE LIFE LINE

For centuries palmists have enjoyed talking about lines on the hand and have given them names and characteristics. Lines are controlled by the nerve endings. They give a physical computer printout of the life and development of each one of us. The lines show our order of priorities and the value that we award ourselves and also our activities. They pick out the environmental influences upon us, add our reaction to those around us, and indicate the depth of the feelings we have toward our mate, family, and friends. They display our dedication to a career or job, as well as our ability to handle it.

We have already talked about the mount of Venus, the area that is enclosed by the life line—but what about the life line itself? It can wrap around Venus or reach out toward the middle of the hand. It can be forked at the end with one branch wrapping around and the other reaching out or make any variety of other shapes. Let us consider these one by one.

A long life line that bows out and forms a large mount of Venus indicates passion and a desire to live life to the full—but the downside is that this person likes his own way and is inclined to have a bad temper. If the line is straighter and creates a smaller Venus mount, the individual is softer, less passionate, and more even-tempered. He spends more time thinking and dreaming than making things happen or putting much energy into making money. If the line rounds the base of the thumb, then home life and possessions are important. This person may strive to live close to his job or even at his place of work.

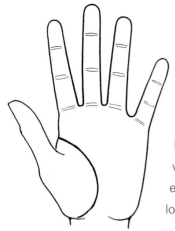

This person is interested in his home and family life. He is not particularly interested in travel or in making his mark in the world, although this depends upon the height of the mount of Venus, because it suggests that he will put in the effort needed to make the money he wants. A woman with this kind of life line may be the earth-mother type, growing her own vegetables and looking after the home and family.

A widely curving life line

A Traveling Line

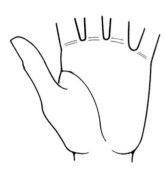

When the line travels out into the hand toward Luna, the person is work-oriented and may travel for business or pleasure. He will meet many people during the course of his work, which may be for the benefit of strangers or the public. He will also use his creativity, imagination, and intuition as part of his job.

Forked Lines

A traveling line

Most people have some kind of fork at the end of the life line—and that is when the line is in one piece in the first place. A fork indicates a combination of home life, career, travel, and a variety of outside interests.

A narrow fork means that there is a long struggle to cope with two demands at once. A typical scenario is that of a woman who brings up children alone. This kind of fork is sometimes so long and narrow that it almost becomes a double life line.

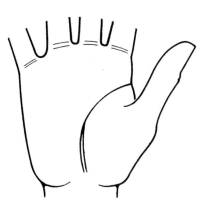

Life is a struggle
for this person

Short life lines are a common feature, and some parts of them are frequently absorbed into part of the fate line. Alternatively, they stop and then start again farther down the hand.

Check for trauma, divorce, redundancy, a change of country, or some other major event. If a new piece of line appears lower down on the hand, this shows that the subject's life is settling down again or that he is getting back on his feet. This can indicate recovery from a long illness, alcoholism, or drug addiction.

This is not a sign of
early death

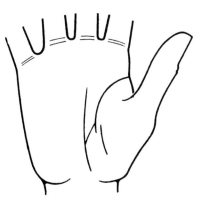

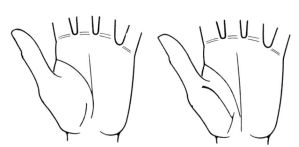

A disturbed life line means a change in fortunes

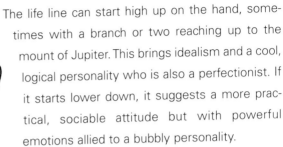

The Starting Point

The life line can start high up on the hand, sometimes with a branch or two reaching up to the mount of Jupiter. This brings idealism and a cool, logical personality who is also a perfectionist. If it starts lower down, it suggests a more practical, sociable attitude but with powerful emotions allied to a bubbly personality.

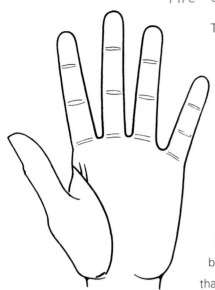

An idealist and perfectionist

If the start of the line is messy, the person's early life is difficult. Islands here can indicate early health problems or emotional traumas. (Check the base of the fate line for confirmation.) A fine line that falls down from the life line in this area can denote the loss of a loved one—through divorce, death, or some other circumstance—in childhood or youth.

A quick guide to timing of youthful events is to drop an imaginary line down from the middle of the Saturn finger (the middle finger) to the life line. The section of life line that precedes this point relates to around the first eighteen to twenty-one years of life.

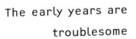

The early years are troublesome

Marks on the Life Line

If you spot a break in the line, an island, a bar that cuts across the line, or any other disturbance, check out both hands because trauma will often show up more strongly on the minor hand than the major one. If such a mark is on both hands, the subject's life will change in practical as well as emotional terms, or there may be a health problem to overcome. A long, narrow island shows a period of deliberate self-sacrifice. This may mean setting aside personal desires for the sake of educating children or working while a partner studies. It simply means that the person puts his own wishes on hold for a longish period. He is also likely to be short of money during this time.

Rising Lines

Lines that rise up from the life line show self-motivation and effort. Note which mount these lines are leading to, as this will indicate what the person is striving to achieve. Lines that fall down show that the subject has given up on something. They can also suggest that a situation has run its course and ended. A rising line often follows an island. This suggests that the subject survives a time of struggle and then makes a successful effort to overcome his problems.

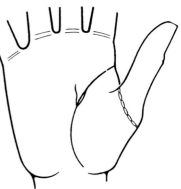

Making a fresh start after a tough time

Shadow Lines

Palmists have different names for these lines—the line of Mars, the median line, sister lines, shadow lines, and so on. Sometimes there are two well-defined lines behind the life line; some palmists call one the line of Mars and the other the median line. This gets so complicated that even I tend to call these shadow lines and leave it at that.

Shadow lines offer protection from illness and accidents, and people who have them are less inclined than others to fall sick or to catch viruses. These lines can also indicate

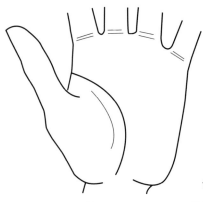

Shadow lines are welcome signs

spiritual protection, a spiritual pathway—or, oddly, a life in the armed services.

Tiny pits on the life line tell us that something is wrong with the spine or its surrounding muscles, ligaments, and tissues. Slipped discs and other such problems are a common cause. Pits close to the start of the line show that the neck is the problem area, and the problem moves down according to the position of the pits. Pits around the lower end of the line signify problems with the hips and legs and the lumbar or sacral area of the spine.

The End of the Line

The life line may end abruptly, it may form tassels, or it may just fizzle out. An abrupt ending suggests that the person will be strong and fit right up to the end, while the other two scenarios signify failing health for some years before life ends. It is wise to check the top of the hands immediately beneath the fingers. Lines that reach up toward the fingers suggest that the person will have a long life. If there is nothing marked, it may be because the person is young and these lines have yet to develop.

THE HEAD LINE

The head line is associated with the way a person's mind works, his aptitudes, education, and career path, and to some extent, financial matters. The head line starts on the thumb side of the hand and travels more or less across the palm. The position of the starting and ending points can

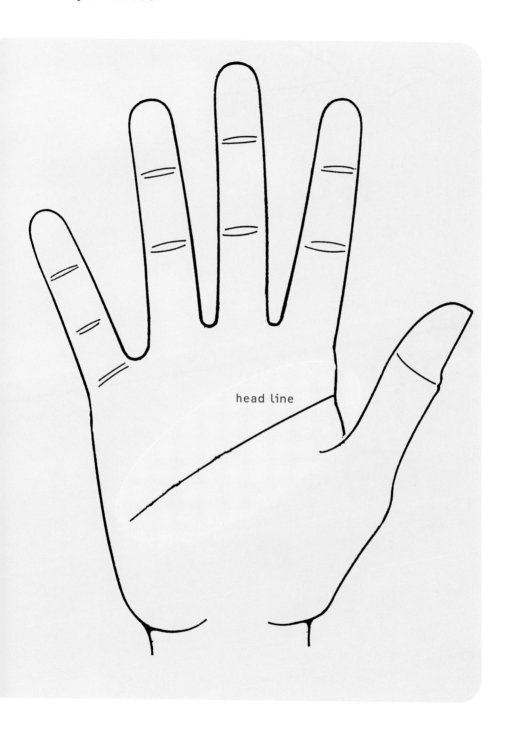

head line

vary enormously and still be normal. When the life line is weak but the head line is strong, the person can overcome weak health or other problems.

The Start of the Head Line

The head line starts from the thumb side of the hand and may join the life line or may be independent of it. It then runs across the hand horizontally or diagonally.

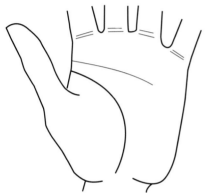

Tied and free head lines

Old-time palmists claimed that a head line that is tied to the life line at the start means that the individual is slow to grow up and stand on his own two feet, while a wide gap between the head and life lines means that he thinks for himself and is also independent in practical terms while relatively young. This doesn't seem to be borne out by fact—in that the "tied" person sits at home until he is middle-aged, while the "free" one leaves home while still young. However, what does seem to happen is that the "tied" person's parents dominate him, while the "free" one has an easy relationship with his family along with plenty of mutual respect.

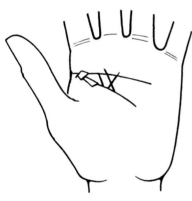

Knitting start to the head and life lines. Early unhappiness

A muddled area that looks like pieces of knitting lying between the head and life line at the point where they part suggests that the subject hated school. Alternatively, he loved it because it represented an escape from a repressive family or domestic difficulties.

Straight, Sloping, and Curved Head Lines

A straight line that travels across the hand goes with a logical mind and an aptitude for mathematics, science, computers, figure work, accountancy, engineering, and similar practical skills. The subject may teach a specialized subject. (Check also for a high mount of Jupiter and longish Jupiter and Mercury fingers for teaching ability.)

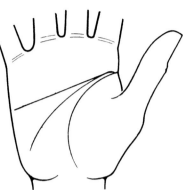

The head line can be straight or curved

When the line is straight and short, we are looking at someone who is immersed in a particular subject—this is a real train-spotter type. He will bring his subject of interest into any conversation at the drop of a hat. Another effect of a short head line is that the person cannot be bothered to think or analyze anything and simply plods through life without making any mental effort.

A line that slopes downward toward Luna shows a creative imagination. This subject can succeed in business because he can pool his practical, creative, and imaginative skills and introduce a useful touch of intuition.

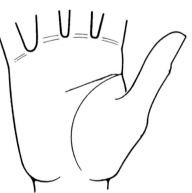

The sign of the specialist

A straight line that suddenly dips downward at the end belongs to a person who loses his temper easily or can be extremely sarcastic.

A long head line signifies a person who never stops learning. If the line is straight, the person may confine his studies to his career, while if it slopes or curves his tastes

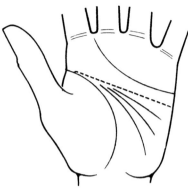

Headlines can curve a
little or a lot

will be more diverse. If the line reaches the percussion, the person will be involved with foreign people and places—possibly in connection with his work.

A curved or sloping head line that leans down toward Luna tells us that the subject has a powerful imagination. This can reveal itself in the way the person thinks, his educational and career choices, or his intuition. He may be interested in travel and exploration or art and creativity. If the line is forked, he will have a talent for writing and he will be versatile. If the line is long, the subject is discriminating and a perfectionist. Curved lines indicate creativity but also sensitivity, moodiness, and depression.

Variations on the Head Line

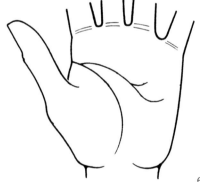

Career and finances
are looking up

A head line that curves up or that throws a little line upward shows an improvement in the person's life, probably due to career or financial improvements. Downward bends and falling lines can indicate losses, but they can also denote jobs or interests that the person discards.

A truly double head line with two distinct starting and ending points is very rare. This person is unlikely to be quite sane. When the secondary line is faint, he may simply have a secondary interest, job, or hobby.

Islands on the head line are a common feature. Chains of small islands suggest that the subject suffers from headaches. An isolated island indicates a career or educational setback, a financial problem, or unhappiness at work. Often this accompanies a feeling of being stuck in the wrong job, the wrong marriage, or the wrong lifestyle. A triangle- or diamond-shaped island can mean actual imprisonment! A deep island that splits the head line into two for part of its journey and then rejoins it suggests mental illness, severe dyslexia, or some other kind of brain impairment.

Note A small island under Saturn can indicate deafness; under Apollo it can indicate eye problems. A series of small islands that look like a skein of wool indicate migraines.

A fork on the head line is known as the writer's fork and is said to show a talent for speech, acting, and writing. Long forks also imply versatility and varied interests, two different part-time jobs, or a hobby or spare-time activity that is different from the day job. Often this person has an ordinary job but is involved in something creative, expressive, or artistic in his spare time. I have seen this on the hand of an accountant who was also a competition ballroom dancer and a homemaker who did something secret in her spare time!

Variety is the spice of life

Breaks in the head line are common. They indicate a career break or even a period away from normal life due to sickness—especially if this affects anything in or around the head area. If there is a break with a square mark around it, the subject will recover completely.

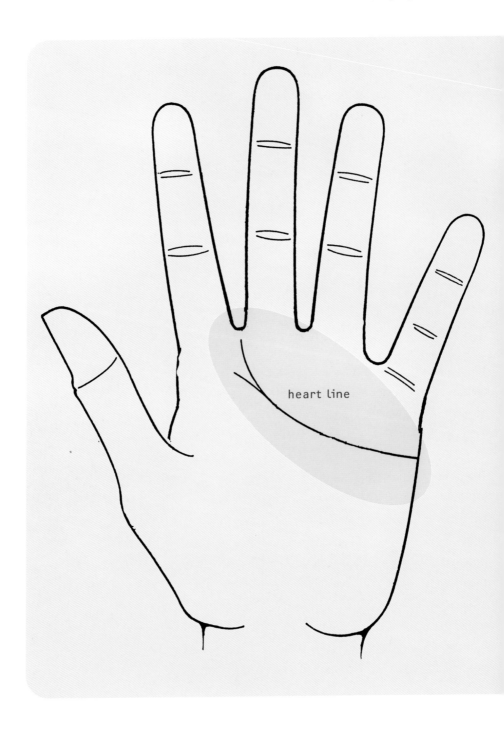

heart line

Long lines that wander across the hand and cross the head line show interference in some aspect of the person's education, career, or life. If these lines come from inside the life line, the family will cause the problem. Short bars indicate short, sharp setbacks.

Too many forks, branches, tassels, islands, breaks, and other disturbances are an indication of a troubled mind or a lifetime of struggle. If the head line is in pieces, the individual will be disorganized. A tassel ending is not a good omen, as it indicates forgetfulness in later life.

THE HEART LINE

The heart line shows how we feel about love and how we behave in connection with love and relationships. It would be nice if it showed the progress of the love life in detail, but it only offers tantalizing glimpses.

The firmer the heart line, the more straightforward the love life. It does not necessarily mean that the individual is any happier than someone whose love life is complicated, but it does show a powerful sense of self-worth and a healthy ego—perhaps a bit too healthy at times! This person receives plenty of love and attention from parents, family, siblings, friends, and partner. He may not be as well loved as he feels himself to be, but he thinks that others consider him wonderful. On the other hand, of course, he may just be a lovely person who is also extremely lucky in love.

Young hands settle down later

Young people often have very flaky or disturbed heart lines, but they settle down later.

The Start of the Line

Some palmists believe that the heart line starts at the percussion edge of the hand, while others see the end that is closer to thumb side as the starting point. I have always used the percussion end as the starting point, so that is how it will be discussed in this book.

Long and Short Heart Lines

A long heart line shows a strong a capacity for affection and friendship, while a short one shows an inward-looking nature with little capacity for love. He could also be very demanding.

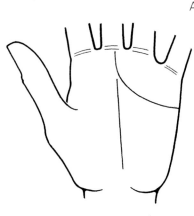

A loving heart

Curved or Straight

A curved heart line shows a capacity for affection. When a relationship breaks up, the subject will become very upset but will soon get over it and move on to a new lover. He follows his heart and believes in romance, and he will happily fall for someone from the wrong side of the tracks, another culture or financial bracket, and so on. Practical considerations are less important to him than the meeting of mind, body, and soul.

This person can be
demanding

A person with a staight heart line selects a lover because she has the right education and comes from the right background or the right financial bracket. He might marry to get on the career ladder, to get into the housing market, or for some other practical reason. The subject has a filter in his mind that automatically rejects an "unsuitable" person to be his wife or the mother of his children. This doesn't mean that he is entirely cynical or that he doesn't love his partner. Indeed, the filter might be subconscious, and he may not be aware of it. When asked, all he will say is that he is choosy. The same person will happily throw away the rule book when it comes to a short-term affair.

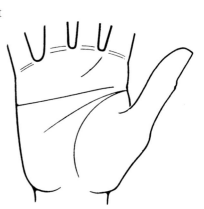

Only the best is
good enough

Bear in mind that while I talk as if I am reading a man's hand in this book, everything applies to both sexes.

A shallow heart line suggests less ability to love, or someone who wants to love but never quite manages to pull it off.

A deep heart line that runs close to the head line can be a sign of intolerance. This person may be demanding, fussy, a perfectionist, or full of rules and regulations. Sometimes severe family problems affect his outlook on life.

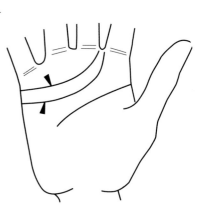

Shallow and deep heart
lines

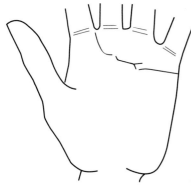

**Fragmented
heart line**

Disturbed Heart Lines

A fragmented heart line can make the subject more successful as a friend than as a partner. This also shows a wonderful sense of humor.

Breaks in the heart line symbolize relationships that end—or heartbreak. Islands usually indicate emotional trouble. Sometimes a clear island under the Apollo finger signifies that a relationship ended abruptly. In some cases, this is due to the sudden death of a partner; in other cases, the partner walks out without giving any warning.

A new piece of line often comes after a break, representing a new relationship. A new piece of line that reaches upward toward the fingers shows that the person will find love later in life. If a tiny double line reaches to the gap between the Jupiter and Saturn fingers, this is definitely the case.

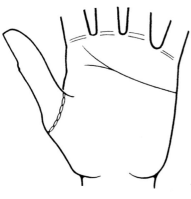

**This person values
his friendships**

The Heart Line in Friendships

Don't forget that love is not only a matter of sexual relationships. It encompasses friendship and fondness for an animal—indeed, any form of affection.

Many people have light lines that fork and fall downward. These forks indicate friendships.

The Mystic Cross

In my early days as a palmist, clients sometimes used to shove a hand out at me and tell me proudly that they had a so-called mystic cross on their palm, indicating psychic gifts. Some palmists say that it does mean this, but only when the cross doesn't touch any other line at all—and that would be extremely unusual. There are other indications of psychism on the hands, though.

Health on the Heart Line

Islands on the heart line can indicate eye problems, dental, lung, or breast problems, and many other conditions. A serious disturbance on an otherwise clear line suggests that something is wrong. A spiky, tasseled, or messy start to the heart line indicates problems with the myocardium or arteries (also check the nails and fingers to see whether they have a blue, violet, or gray tone). Blue pits on the line in the areas below and between Saturn and Mercury can indicate lung problems, while disturbances between Saturn and Jupiter denote breast problems.

Gay or Straight

There is no difference in the heart line of a gay person unless he suffers mental anguish or major family problems. Then the line may throw a strong branch down into the area where the head and life lines start.

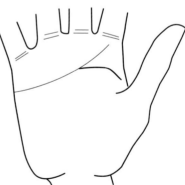

Agonizing over sexuality

SIMIAN AND SEMI-SIMIAN LINES

Sometimes the head and heart lines merge into one strong line that cuts right across the hand, forming a simian line. This line can appear on one or both hands. The simian line is often heavy and chainlike. In many cases, there are semi-simian formations where there are vestigial pieces of head and heart lines left on the hand.

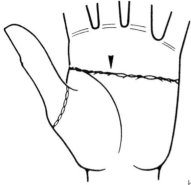

The simian line

The word "simian," meaning "monkeylike," is used because early palmists thought that monkeys had this formation on their hands. I have visited zoos and studied the hands of many apes and monkeys, even going as far as taking handprints from a baby Barbary ape when I was in Gibraltar. I discovered that the lines on any monkey or ape hand are the same as human ones and that these creatures do not have a "simian" line formation. The skin ridge patterns are quite different from those of humans though.

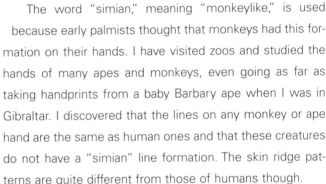

The semi-simian line

People with simian lines find it difficult to lead a normal, balanced life. They focus entirely on either their work or their relationship, or on something else in a one-sided manner. They hold on to resentments and then explode in a tantrum or floods of tears. These people can be very obstinate.

Semi-simian lines are also uncommon. They mean much the same as a simian line, but the person is likely to develop a more balanced attitude with time and experience.

THE FATE LINE

If you learn nothing else about palmistry, try to come to grips with the fate line, because it has so much to tell. Not everybody has a fate line, but if you look closely, you will often see fragments of it somewhere on the hand. The fate line runs vertically up the hand from the bottom to the top. It can start on Neptune (the middle of the base of the hand), or it can start closer to one side or the other.

The fate line can be a partial line that starts and then fizzles out or one that does not start until higher up the hand. The fate line tells two stories, and it is hard to differentiate between them. The first story shows the times when we make an effort in life. The second story is about the amount of fate, destiny, kismet, karma, and luck a person will experience—and when this will occur. It shows the benefits and challenges that we will have in relationships, finances, family, career, and much else. This line can change quite a lot at times, so even bad things are not set in stone. Make an effort to improve your circumstances and your lines will change!

Note This is sometimes called the Saturn line, because it is supposed to run toward the Saturn finger, but it can hive off toward the Jupiter or Apollo finger instead, so we will stick with the old name, the fate line.

If there is no fate line, the person will not make much of an effort in life. A very strong, deeply marked line shows that the person will do what others tell him to. He may feel that he has a duty to his parents, job, spouse, or family.

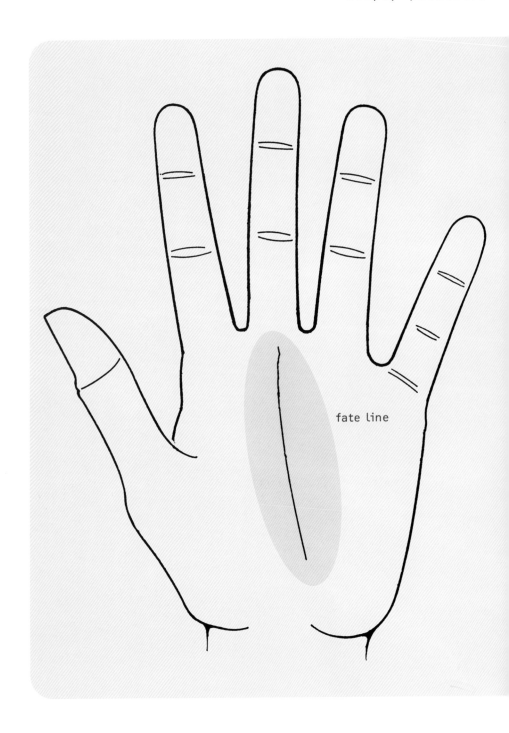

fate line

However, this is not all bad news, because he will make a success of whatever comes along. At least this fate line indicates that something happens in his life, and he can be quite ambitious too.

The Start of the Fate Line

Here are some quick clues to the meaning of the start of the line.

The line rises on Neptune—self-motivation and making one's own decisions early in life.

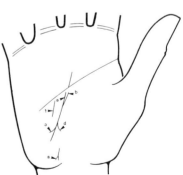

Fate line running toward Saturn

The line rises on the Venus side, from the life line or from within the life line. The family will help this person to get on in life—perhaps by paying for him to go to a good school or helping him to set up a home or a business. The person's family thinks well of him. The closer the line is to Venus, the more likely the individual will cling to his family when he becomes an adult. His family may dictate to him: he may like it that way or he may just put up with it.

The line rises from Luna. The subject will have help, acceptance, esteem, and recognition from outsiders rather than from the family. The closer the starting point is to Luna, the more likely it is that he will strike out on his own early in life.

Fate line variations

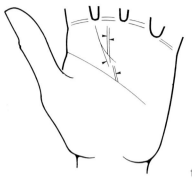

This person finds his way only later in life

Sometimes the line only starts higher up on the hand. When the line starts at the head line, a lucky break may jump-start a career, or tough circumstances will encourage this person to make an extra effort.

When the line starts at the heart line, it may be love that makes the difference. This also suggests that the subject's later years will be happier and more interesting than his early ones.

The Direction of the Fate Line

The fate line can fade out halfway up the hand, which means that a period of effort ends. Partial fate lines can reappear farther up the hand, showing a change in fortune. Here are a few more pointers:

The line runs toward Jupiter, showing that the subject will put his heart into a career. If the fate line joins the heart line at the end, the subject may put his career before his love life.

The fate line heads toward Saturn. The subject will always work hard and may be very successful later in life.

The fate line ends between Saturn and Apollo. The subject will be happy later in life and able to spend money on luxuries and pleasures as well as necessities.

Timing on the Fate Line

Here is a rough way to work out dates on the fate line:

Take something—a piece of string—and run it across the hand from the middle of the knuckle that lies at the base of the thumb. Look at the point at which the thread crosses the fate line. This represents the period around the age of twenty-three to twenty-five. Remember the following:

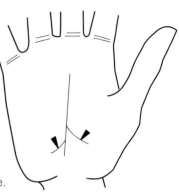

Important new people

- ◆ The fate line crosses the head line at the age of around thirty to thirty-five.

- ◆ The fate line crosses the heart line at around age forty-five to fifty.

- ◆ You can see the remaining years in the small area above the heart line.

Lines Joining the Fate Line

Branches that join the fate line indicate friends, lovers, marriage partners, mentors in business, financial partners, and many others who become part of the subject's life for a while. The usual scenario is love or marriage.

A relationship will start at the age of the joint, but if it crosses over the line or runs with it for a while and then leaves, the relationship will not last.

A relationship will endure if a line joins the fate line and then becomes part of it.

A line joins the fate line from the thumb side of the hand. The lover will come from the same neighborhood and background as the subject. He and his family may know the lover before the couple gets together. Both lovers will have a similar culture, ambitions, and outlook on life.

When the joining line comes from the Luna side, the lover or person of influence comes from afar or from a different environment.

When a relationship breaks up, you may be able to work out whether the lover goes back to Mother (the joining line leaves on the Venus side) or leaves the area (the joining line leaves on the Luna side).

Events on the Fate Line

Any disturbance to the fate line is interesting. Here are a few possibilities:

- ◆ An isolated island means a period of confusion and unhappiness. See whether this happens in childhood, youth, or later.

- ◆ In adult life, an isolated island often represents a shortage of money for a few years.

- ◆ A long island that splits the line in two for part of its route suggests that the person is torn in two directions or trying to cope with two different situations at once, such as a busy home life caring for children, plus a tough career.

Bars, breaks, crosses, or any other kind of confusion on the line denote setbacks. This can refer to career or financial setbacks, but health problems, divorce, or almost anything else could apply. This is an instance in which you have to look around the hand for more information.

Confusion in early years

Moving Fate Lines

Sometimes the fate line breaks and a new piece forms slightly higher up the hand. This new piece may "jump" toward the radial or ulna side of the original line, and it might even run parallel to the original for part of its route. In this case, the individual will start something new while he is still in his previous situation. For example, he may start a business while still working at his job, or he may start a new relationship before leaving his previous one. If the new piece of line does not overlap, there will be a break between the past life and the new one.

There will be less interest in work and more interest in home life if the new line jumps to the ulna side. The person may change his job to be closer to home or he may give up a demanding job for a lighter one—alternatively he may marry or decide to take more interest in the home and family. When the line jumps to the radial side, the subject becomes more interested in work and less interested in home life.

Choosing work over family life

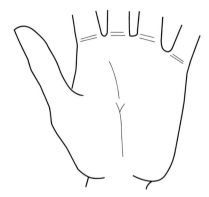

Suddenly walking out

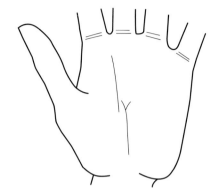

Making plans and then
suddenly walking out

Sometimes the line breaks up into a number of little lines that resemble a small forest rather than a clear line. In this case, the person will become self-employed and thus have a great variety of tasks to cope with. He may put great bursts of energy into something at this point.

Sometimes the fate line comes to an abrupt end, leaving a gap before a new piece of line forms a little further up the hand. If the ending shows a small "Y" formation, the person will suddenly walk out of a job or project, leave a relationship, or even leave the country! This may appear to be a sudden impulse, but it has been coming for a long time. If a new section of line starts to rise up the hand—beside the bit that ends in the "Y"—the person will plan the break in advance, perhaps by looking for a new career direction before making the break.

The End of the Fate Line

Here are some of the many meanings attached to the end of the fate line:

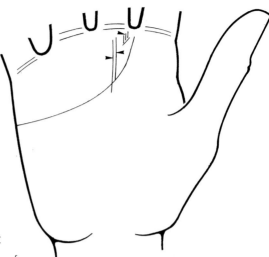

See how life works out for you in the end

◆ If the line reaches the mount of Saturn, the person will work almost to the end of his life, and he may enjoy doing so. (See also the loop of serious intent in the skin ridge pattern chapter of this book.) The chances are that he will make a success of his career and have enough money to live comfortably later in life.

◆ If the line ends on Jupiter, the subject will achieve personal fulfillment through a career, a religious way of life, or some other activity that gives him satisfaction.

◆ If the line heads toward Apollo, he will probably end up with a nice home and a happy family.

◆ If the line doesn't reach far above the heart line, the person may simply give up and become a couch potato.

7

THE MINOR LINES

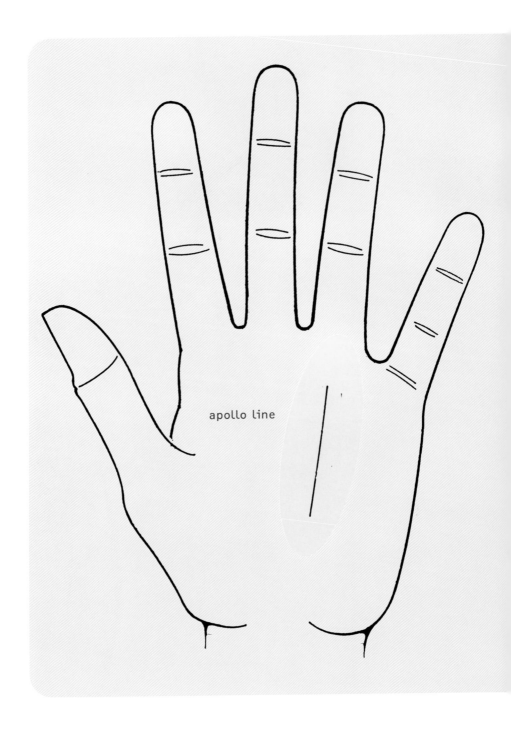

apollo line

We have looked at the four major lines: life, head, heart, and fate, and even the strange simian line, but now let us consider some of the many minor lines.

THE APOLLO LINE

Some palmists call this line the Sun line, but most call it the Apollo line because it travels up the hand toward the Apollo finger. Not everybody has an Apollo line, and even when it is present, it is rarely complete. This line is concerned with family life, fun, pleasure, and creativity and denotes fame and recognition. In the lives of normal people, it often has something to say about the home, family circumstances, and property matters.

The Start of the Apollo Line

The line usually starts low on the hand—on Luna, Neptune, or somewhere in that area. It can start close to the fate line, but it often glides in from somewhere on the Luna mount.

When the line starts toward the center of the lower part of the hand, around the mount of Neptune, there will be a helping hand from family or from family connections in the subject's early days. If a branch enters it from the radial side at this lower end, this is even more likely. The person's family might be instrumental in helping him to buy his first home or make an early start on setting up a family.

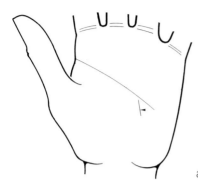

Who will help you to succeed?

More often, this line starts on the mount of Luna. This suggests that the person gets his breaks from people and situations outside the home or by using his own imagination or intuition. The imaginative, creative, and artistic aspects of a person's nature may please and impress his family, but the only place to obtain credibility (and payment) for creative talents is in the world outside the home.

An Apollo line that starts below the head line shows early promise. When it starts farther up the hand, the individual may not settle into a home or family life until later.

Events

◆ Many of the same conditions that we see on the fate line apply to the Apollo line. Here are some common scenarios:

◆ Doubled lines imply a split in terms of time and energy.

◆ A break followed by a new line signifies a change of career and/or a change of address. A line that breaks and jumps toward the ulna side puts the emphasis on home life.

◆ A radial jump takes the person out of the home and into the world.

◆ If this line draws other fine lines toward it at some point, the subject may start to work from home or look for a creative outlet.

◆ For most people, the Apollo line is concerned less with becoming famous than with setting up a home. Use the same information as in the fate line and apply it to property matters. For instance, an island on the line, a bar, a break, or any other disturbance will cause problems related to buying or selling a property.

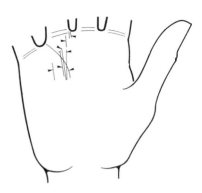

Happiness in later life

The End of the Apollo Line

Most people have some part of an Apollo line, but it may only start above the heart line, running up to the fingers. This is a nice thing to see, because it shows happiness in later life. It may also indicate an interest in sports or creative pursuits when the need to earn a living has passed. A trident is a three-pronged ending to the Apollo line. This lucky symbol shows that the person will always be able to wriggle out of money problems—possibly more by luck than by judgment.

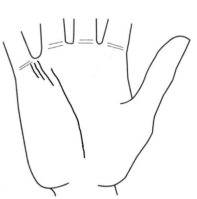

Ladder of success

If this line ends in a "ladder of success," which is a series of little lines that creep up the top end of the hand, with each step getting closer to the Mercury finger, this suggests achievement and satisfaction later in life.

HEALTH LINES

If the health line is present, the person is interested in health and healing. He may be interested in his own state of health or that of his family and friends. Alternatively, he

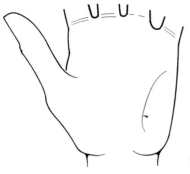

Curved health line

may work in the health field, or in spiritual healing, psychology, counseling, or channeling.

Look for red marks or little pits on the line, because these occur when someone is likely to be unwell—even if he is unaware of the impending ailment.

When a line curves around the percussion side of the hand, regardless of whether it ends up on Mercury or not, the subject is extremely intuitive and probably psychic.

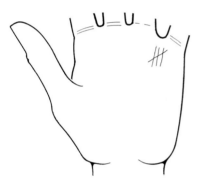

A talent for healing

The health line often ends in three little lines with a diagonal line through them. This section of the line becomes the healing striate, or healing lines.

Health and healing are so important to this subject that he could work in the field of health. This can include anything that aids the mental and physical health of people or animals. The healing can be practical, spiritual, or psychological. This mark is commonly found on the hands of palmists, because we try to help those who are worried or unhappy.

TRAVEL LINES

Travel lines enter the hand from the percussion edge and show important journeys and connections with people in other countries. If one of these lines reaches out across the hand and touches the fate or life line, it suggests an important connection to someone or somewhere overseas. The individual may even spend a few years abroad at some point

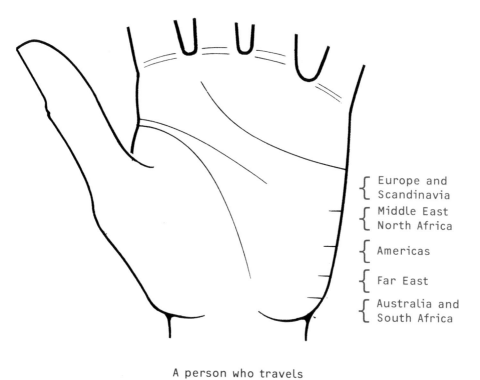

Europe and
Scandinavia
Middle East
North Africa
Americas
Far East
Australia and
South Africa

A person who travels

in his life. A skilled palmist can tell which countries the person will visit.

Strong lines show important connections and trips; fainter ones might just be pleasant vacations. The list of correspondences that follows applies to everybody, wherever the person happens to have been born:

◆ Between the heart and head line: Scandinavia and Europe

◆ Around the end of the head line: the Mediterranean, Eastern Europe, and the Middle East

◆ Long straight lines on Mars/Luna: the United States, Canada, the Caribbean and South America, Russia

◆ Mid-Luna: India, Pakistan, Sri Lanka, Seychelles, other Gulf States, Asian countries

◆ Lower Luna: China, Korea, Japan

◆ Pluto: Australia, South Africa, New Zealand

Disturbances on the travel lines will mean:

◆ Island: Problem trip, possibly due to illness while traveling

◆ Break: Broken journey

◆ Double: Two journeys in quick succession

◆ Disturbed or frayed: A bothersome trip or a wasted journey

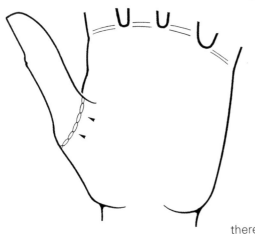

FAMILY LINE

Just at the point where the thumb joins the hand, there is a crease. If there is a clean, clear line or even a chained line, the person will live in one house for many years, possibly for life. If it is fragmented, he will move around a lot. If there are extra family lines shadowing the main

one, he may own an extra house, a timeshare, or a
caravan, recreational vehicle, or something
else that he uses or rents out.

THE GIRDLE OF VENUS

The girdle of Venus
shows sensitivity

The girdle of Venus lies beneath the two middle
fingers. Sometimes this girdle is complete, but often it is
broken or only parts of it appear. Either way, the girdle
belongs to a sensitive person who may also be intuitive or
psychic. A partial girdle is nice, because it shows an ability
to make friends easily. A complete girdle can belong to
someone who is so sensitive that he bursts into tears at the
slightest provocation.

Unfortunately, someone who has a fully formed girdle of
Venus can be offensive. He may think he is being defensive,
but those who are on the wrong end of his unpleasantness
don't see it that way.

If the part of the girdle that runs diagonally down and
around from between the Jupiter and Saturn fingers is
present, the person is ambitious in terms of love and career,
and he may want both these aspects of life to be perfect.

If the part of the girdle that runs diagonally down and
around from between the Mercury and Apollo fingers is
present, the person will want to be with others who share
similiar interests. He will have an active mind.

THE RING OF SOLOMON

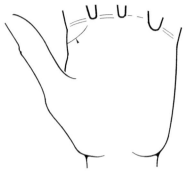

The ring of Solomon belongs to a wise person who can listen to others and give good advice. It is common to see this mark on the hand of counselors, advisers, bank managers, lawyers, social workers, and others who help the public.

On very rare occasions, similar rings appear to "cup" the Saturn or Apollo fingers. These symbolize a blockage of energy up the palm and into the fingers. A ring under the Mercury finger is called the "widow line" for obvious reasons.

The ring of Solomon denotes sympathy

MILITARY LINES

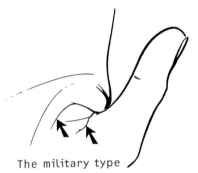

Military lines appear on the area called lower Mars. They show that the individual is suited to pursuing a profession such as youth leader, Scout, paramilitary or paramedical professional, or fire fighter.

The military type

MONEYMAKER LINE

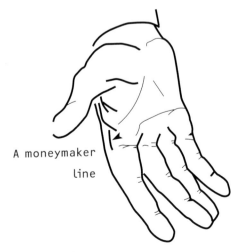

We could all do with this line! It is a fine line running vertically down the radial side of the mount of Jupiter almost at the side of the hand. This line helps the person to pull the irons out of the fire when money runs short.

A moneymaker line

THE VIA LASCIVA OR ALLERGY LINE

This weird line starts on the percussion edge of the hand and runs into the mount of Luna. The old term, via lasciva, meant "lascivious road"— implying that the person was sex-mad and possibly a pervert. This is complete rubbish. A more common situation is that the person suffers from allergies. Allergies and asthma are even more likely to be present when this line is on a hand that has many lines on it.

RASCETTES

Rascettes are the bracelets that appear around the wrist. Old-time palmists used to say that each rascette represents thirty years of life, so if there are three rascettes, the person will live past the age of ninety. This claim is not born out by fact, but when the upper rascette creeps into the hand or is broken up, the subject lacks a strong constitution.

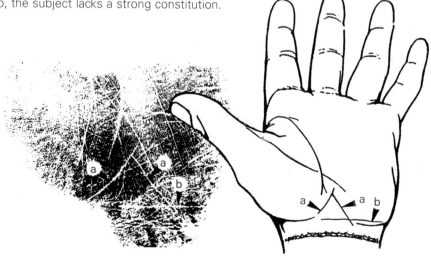

8

LOVE AND RELATIONSHIPS

Attachment lines

Always look at both hands for evidence about the love and relationship lines because the minor hand can often be more revealing and accurate when dealing with this emotive area of a person's life. The attachment lines are little creases that enter the palm horizontally from the percussion edge of the hand in the area between the bottom of the little finger and the heart line. Some old-time palmistry books say that these lines show how many children a person will have, but this is not so.

The lines refer to adult relationships. In the old days, this meant marriage—but hands do not register marriage certificates, so these lines refer to relationships that we feel strongly about. Sometimes a marriage may register a faint or stunted line, while an affair can deposit a disproportionately heavy one.

One really hot tip is to focus on the color of these lines and the area surrounding them. If it is the same as the rest of the hand, changes are unlikely to occur in the short term. However, if there is redness, dark coloration, or many little muddled lines in the area, the subject could be very unhappy about the state of his relationship to the point where something dramatic is likely to happen.

There may be one strong line, two lines, more than two, or a number of strong lines with perhaps a few vague ones as well. These lines can appear, disappear, and change their appearance very rapidly. It would be nice to say that one line means one attachment, two means two, and so on, but this area of hand reading is all about feelings. It concerns the contents of a person's head and heart rather than concrete facts. You will see what I mean as we go through this chapter.

Although there is no hard and fast rule, I have found that it works well if you read attachment lines by starting with the lowest and working upward. The lowest line often symbolizes the first important relationship, with later ones coming in turn as you climb up toward the base of the Mercury finger.

In theory, one strong attachment line means one long partnership, but it can also show what the subject wants in an ideal world. If a relationship fails, this person will try to find another and make that one work. This person is romantic rather than calculating. He is loving and giving and not particularly cautious and self-preserving. He (or, more likely, she) buys into the romantic ideal of finding a soul mate or falling into the arms of an understanding lover who supplies every emotional need. If this person is lucky, the first and only relationship is wonderful and endures. The subject marries and lives happily ever after. As you can imagine, it is rare for anyone to attain this ideal—but the line shows that this is what the person wants, and what he will try to achieve.

If such a subject has more than one relationship during his lifetime, he will probably concentrate on only one of these at a time. Thus, if there is an affair during the course of a marriage, the affair will count more than the marriage itself in emotional terms. If this individual loses a lover, he will not forget the past love, but he will go on, in due course, to love again. In many cases, a faint additional line will appear above the original one later on.

When there are two attachment lines, the individual weighs up his relationship rather than simply trying to make the best of a bad job. He will question whether he really wants to stay in the partnership forever. He may not admit this openly, but somewhere deep inside him, there is a small voice telling him that his marriage is not right. Two marriages are a strong possibility here.

Young people often display several faint lines while they are still playing the field or looking around. The same can arise in a longish period between partnerships. In this case, it is best to concentrate on any lines that stand out. If no line really stands out, the person is not yet ready to settle down. Later on, some of the lines will fade away and one or two stronger ones will emerge.

CONCERNING THE RELATIONSHIP

Death of a current or former partner

There are many factors to look at here, and some are not pleasant. Here is the worst-case scenario—that of foretelling the death of a partner.

The attachment line becomes deeper and slightly chained and turns up to touch the crease at the base of the Mercury finger, or there is a separate ring under the Mercury finger. In this case, the person will lose a partner through death. This mark seems to form on the hands a few years before the death occurs. I have seen this in the case of people who have left a partner, moved on to another, and then heard that the previous partner has died.

EASY AND CHALLENGING RELATIONSHIPS

Now let's look at the illustrations and see what they tell us. The first illustration shows two lines. One line is straight and the other line bends downward. A person can have one line, which can be perfectly straight or may curve downward. He may have two lines, one of which is straight and the other curved. The variations are enormous.

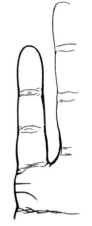

In this illustration, the straight line belongs to the person who wants (or has) one good relationship that exists for a long time. The bent line shows a similarly long relationship, but the individual will become depressed at times because he is put upon, used, or even bullied by his partner.

Easy and difficult relationships

In the next illustration, there is one line that turns upward and one that has a little fork at the end. The line that turns upward suggests that the subject's partner is successful in his field and that he or she may be wealthy. In this case, look for a cross on the mount of Jupiter, as that also signifies marrying money. The forked line shows a marriage or relationship that comes to a sudden end.

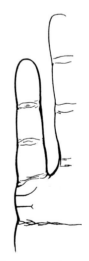

An island on an attachment line suggests that the partner is sick or is likely to become sick soon. Alternatively, the partner may have financial, business, or other problems on his mind at the time of the reading. This is a warning to keep an eye on the partner for a while.

An upward curve brings a successful partner. A short, sharp fork shows a sudden split in a relationship

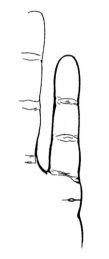

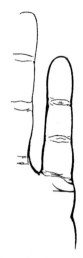

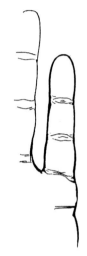

A sick or worried
partner

This relationship
is in trouble

Parallel lives

A forked line or a frayed line suggests that the relationship is experiencing difficulties.

Parallel lines suggest that the partners coexist in the same house but that the marriage is not emotionally satisfying.

A line that forks or doubles at the percussion edge but which then blends into one line shows a strong element of friendship in the marriage. It is possible that the partners started out as friends before getting together.

A line that has a finer companion line above or beneath suggests that the person has other interests apart from the partner. Many things could come between the subject and his lover, but an affair outside marriage is a common scenario.

I have a funny story to tell here. Many years ago, I took a course that qualified me to teach adults in any adult education institute in the world. The people in the course hoped to teach anything from cookery to flower arranging, picture framing, office skills, car maintenance, care for the elderly, and many other nonacademic subjects. Needless to say, I wanted to teach astrology and palmistry. Toward the end of the course, we all had to make some kind of presentation. Some used practical, hands-on techniques, while others used various different methods that we had learned along the way. We did our presentations in front of the students and the various teachers who worked in the course. It fell to me to use an overhead projector for my presentation, so I decided to ask a guinea pig to allow me to take a handprint, and I used that for my presentation. One of the teachers offered his hand for the reading, but I doubt whether he realized just how detailed palmistry would be in the hands of an expert.

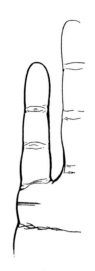

An outside interest

I started my presentation by going through the lines one by one, and soon I was lost in my art and oblivious of the effect that my reading might be having on my audience or my guinea pig. Eventually I came to his attachment lines. I remarked on the companion line alongside his main attachment line and commented that he was very likely embroiled in an affair that was a danger to his marriage. Up to this point, my audience had been listening quietly and attentively, but then there was a sudden communal intake of breath. I turned to the teacher in question and noticed that his face was as white as a sheet. Unbeknown to me, he was in the throes of a passionate affair with another staff member. Shortly after this revelation, he dropped her and went back to his wife. Oh dear!

Now, let us get back to the business in hand—so to speak.

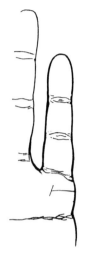

If a deletion line appears close to an attachment line, or if it runs through the attachment line, the marriage is wedged so far on the rocks that a split is likely.

A square over an attachment line can mean restriction, but it can also signify that the partner is protected while in a difficult or dangerous situation.

CHILD LINES

This relationship is over

Child lines run vertically through the attachment lines. They can be on the percussion edge just where it curves around to the palm or just into the palm. These are difficult for even a good palmist to judge, as they are often very fine and difficult to see. Try sprinkling a little talcum powder on this area of the hand, because that will make these lines stand out clearly. A child line should cut through at least one of the attachment lines.

Generally, one line means one child, two means two children, and so on. Straight lines can refer to sons, while sloping ones tend to refer to daughters. However, this can refer to the nature of the child, because a gentle, artistic boy will sometimes show up as a sloping line and vice versa. When child lines are close together, the children are close in age. A gap may show that the children are dissimilar to each other or that there is a gap in their ages.

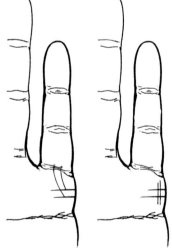

Child lines   Child lines
(girls)   (boys)

Sometimes a subject has these lines but doesn't have children. In this case, ask if he or she looks after children or teaches them, because someone who enjoys being with children may have many fine lines here. The same goes for someone who brings up children that are not his own. This can also apply to a person who cares for animals.

Disturbances on Child Lines

◆ The rules for disturbances on the child lines are similar to those for any other line. Here are a few common scenarios:

◆ A child line with an island suggests that a child is sick or troubled in some way.

◆ If the child line is split, has a deletion line across it, or any other disturbance, it is worth asking the subject what (if anything) is wrong either with the child or between the parents and the child.

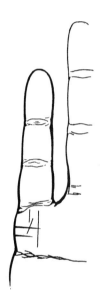

◆ Lines that fizzle out, with or without an island showing on them, or lines that wriggle and wander but do not go far enough to cut through an attachment line can indicate miscarriages or abortions.

One of many kinds of disturbances on a child line

◆ Sometimes a perfectly normal line can also indicate a child who did not make it into life for some reason.

SIBLING LINES

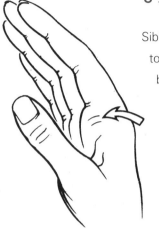

Sibling lines

Sibling lines refer to brothers and sisters. They can also refer to cousins, neighbors, and good friends who feel like brothers and sisters. These are on the opposite side of the hand from attachment lines. There are some clues that you can pick up from these lines.

◆ Straight lines equal happy siblings.

◆ A line curving upward equals a very happy and successful sibling.

◆ A line curving downward suggests an unhappy sibling.

◆ A square on a sibling line represents protection in a difficult situation.

◆ A star or discoloration suggests a temporary problem for the sibling.

INTERFERENCE LINES

Lines that interfere

Unless a person decides to be a recluse or a hermit, life will be full of relationships of one kind or another, and there are many features on a hand that talk of our connection with other people. One that is worth looking out for is a stray line or two—or sometimes a whole bunch of them—that reach out from the mount of Venus and wander across the hand. These are interference lines. They show how we allow parents, partners, and others to cramp our style and dictate to us. If you see such lines, trace their path and see which area of the hand and which lines they cross. This will show the areas that are being restricted or affected by the dictatorial or meddling person.

CUPID'S ARROW—OR SOMETHING TO THAT EFFECT...

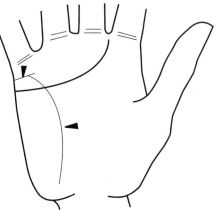

It is possible to fall in love with someone in an instant—indeed many passionate attractions start in just that way. The *coup de foudre*, the meeting with a stranger that turns our knees to jelly and that soon becomes a matter of heated desire, passion, pain, ecstasy, and so on, is a rare but unforgettable experience. The clue to this is when the line of health connects with one of the attachment lines. Perhaps this means that a traumatic affair can be bad for one's health?

A passionate love affair

9

MARKS

Marks come and go according to the subject's current situation at the time of the reading.

THE SQUARE

The square often appears on the mount of Jupiter, where it acts as a form of protection to the person as a whole. This subject will recover from setbacks. An isolated square on a line sometimes surrounds a break or an island. It acts as a protection against accident, injury, or major loss.

- ◆ If the square is on the life line, the problem is spinal.

- ◆ If the square is on the head line, the problem is with the head.

- ◆ If the square is on the heart line, the problem is with the upper part of the body.

- ◆ If there is a square but not an island or break, the subject is being restricted.

- ◆ If the square is on the life line, the restriction is general.

- ◆ If the square is on the head line, the restriction is educational, mental, or career-related.

- ◆ If the square is on the heart line, the subject's partner is restricting him.

◆ If the square is on the fate line, the restriction could be almost anything.

THE CROSS AND THE STAR

A cross on Luna seems to indicate an important voyage on or over water. Someone once told me that a person with a cross on the mount of Luna would never suffer from seasickness. On the odd occasions when I have come across this unusual mark, I asked whether the people got sick on boats and they replied that they did not, so there must be something in this.

Crosses on Apollo seem to mean winning something—perhaps a lottery or raffle. This also often relates to money that drifts in later, such as royalties. A series of crosses running down fairly close to the center of the hand link with those who work in large organizations that have many rooms, such as hospitals, schools, or large office blocks. I guess one would see this on most hands in New York or central London!

A star signifies a temporary problem, so look at the mount and line concerned to see what this might be.

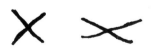

MORE MINOR MARKS

◆ A triangle signifies talent.

◆ A diamond suggests feelings of imprisonment.

◆ Stray lines indicate interference by others.

◆ A tasseled line suggests vitamin deficiency or worry.

A grille always indicates sickness. The area of the hand will give you a clue as to what the sickness relates to. Some years ago, I had "women's trouble" that resulted in a hysterectomy. While I was sick, for several months after the operation, the lower part of my right hand was almost obliterated by a network of fine lines that formed a huge grille. Once I recovered, the grille became less overpowering, but it has never completely gone away.

Dots or tiny pits on any line are important because they indicate the sudden onset of an ailment. I remember on one occasion, when my first husband developed a kidney stone a deep pit suddenly appeared on his health line and stayed there for a while. The pit went away again once he passed the stone and his kidney recovered.

SKIN RIDGE PATTERNS

We are familiar with the idea of skin ridge patterns in the form of fingerprints, but these patterns also occur on other parts of a hand. Skin ridge patterns form at around eight to nine weeks of gestation and stay with us throughout life, but they can change their appearance due to age and deteriorating health. Psoriasis will affect the appearance of the fingers and their ridge patterns. With what I know about hands, it amazes me that the police and immigration authorities place so much faith in fingerprints.

While it is true that the skin ridge patterns on the fingers and the hands do not change, age and sickness can all but obliterate them. The patterns change when we are sick or exhausted. If we take a break or if life gets back on track, the ridges will repair themselves. Fingerprints become muddy when we get old, and they can almost disappear in the case of partially sighted or blind people. Alcoholism and drug addiction will affect the skin ridge patterns on the palms and make the long lines break down into "strings of pearls," especially on the mount of Luna.

We believe that fingerprints are unique to each person, but there have been cases of wrongful conviction on fingerprint evidence. No two people can have a full set of identical prints—not even identical twins—but one finger can carry a print that is so close to a complete stranger's that they are almost a perfect match.

Looped skin ridge patterns

On the palm rather than the fingertips, most hands have at least one loop somewhere. The most common is the loop of humor. Sometimes these loops can be quite small, so it is worth taking a close look at the hand to see if you can spot them.

The loop is by far the most common mark, but a loop can contain a small whorl or peacock's eye within it.

◆ The rajah loop is at the top of the palm between the mounts of Jupiter and Saturn. It is an unusual mark that signifies royal blood, especially when it appears on both hands.

◆ The loop of serious intent is at the top of the palm between the mounts of Saturn and Apollo. It belongs to a hard worker and a deep thinker.

◆ The loop of humor is located at the top of the hand between the mounts of Apollo and Mercury. It is a lovely sign that signifies a sense of humor and a love for animals.

◆ The loop of style is found in the same area as the loop of humor, but it often leans toward the mount of Apollo. This shows a sense of style and a touch of glamor.

◆ The memory loop is on, or close to, the end of the head line. It shows that the subject has a good memory. A salesperson who remembers people's names, details of the products he or she sells, and prices will have a memory loop.

◆ The countryside loop comes from the percussion side of the hand and lands on the mount of Luna. This loop denotes a love of the countryside and possibly the sea.

There is another mark, called a tri-radius. This means three arms or radii. Swaths of skin ridges pass by a part of the palm and coincidentally make a triangle that may be slightly prominent. Some palmists believe that the position of a tri-radius can show a tendency to heart disease, but I have not found the tri-radius mark to be of any importance.

The tri-radius

10

HEALTH ON THE HANDS

This is such a vast subject that it can easily fill a book all by itself. For those who are especially interested in diagnosis, complementary therapies, or other health matters, this is the most exciting and interesting aspect of hand reading. For the rest of us, it is a fascinating part of the subject as a whole. There are a few books that specialize in this aspect of palmistry, so if it particularly interests you, look on Amazon.com or Amazon.co.uk for them. My own advanced book, *Modern Palmistry*, has a large section on health. This was mainly because my coauthor, a spiritual healer, was very interested in health matters.

Older readers may actually have visited doctors who checked the fingernails for anemia by pressing down on a nail, then seeing how long it took the blood to return. Doctors also used the nails and hands to check for psoriasis, kidney failure, tuberculosis, and many other ailments, but modern doctors no longer use this kind of diagnosis. Whenever I point out how much information is available on hands, medical professionals are amazed and fascinated.

GENERAL APPEARANCE

Soft hands belong to those who want an easy life, but they can also be an indication of sickness or thyroid problems, especially if the skin feels like cellophane stretched over a gel filling. Softness also occurs during pregnancy and in the hands of vegetarians, so it seems to signify a low level of iron in the blood.

◆ Hot, sweaty hands signify possible thyroid or glandular disorders.

◆ Hot, dry hands can indicate blood pressure or kidney disorders or fever.

◆ Cold hands indicate poor circulation, shock, or fever.

◆ Clammy hands denote a sluggish liver.

◆ Cold patches suggest uneven circulation due to heart disorders, especially when some parts of the fingers are warm and others are cool.

COLOR

If a hand changes color, it can indicate a health problem. Here are a few common ones:

red: a smoker or ex-smoker

pale: poor circulation or anemia

bluish/lilac/gray: heart trouble

yellow: liver trouble

THE LINES

Tiny pits along the life line indicate backache, slipped discs, and other spinal problems. If the problem is in the neck area, these appear on the upper part of the line. If the lumbar region is painful, the pits show up much further down the line, beside or around the mount of Venus.

Chains on the head line indicate headaches or migraine. Islands on the head or the heart line can relate to problems with the eyes, ears, or head. A break can indicate a head injury. A truly strange head line with huge islands is a sign of mental illness. A strange formation on the percussion that looks like a pair of tongs grabbing the end of the head line relates to insomnia.

Flakiness at the start of the heart line under the Mercury mount is a sign of heart trouble. Any disturbance or island under Saturn or Jupiter, where the line starts to bend upward, is an indication of breast problems. Feathering along the line can mean a shortage of potassium, which leads to depression.

Dots, pits, blue marks, grilles, discoloration, redness, or anything else that is strange on any line can mean inflammation in some area of the body.

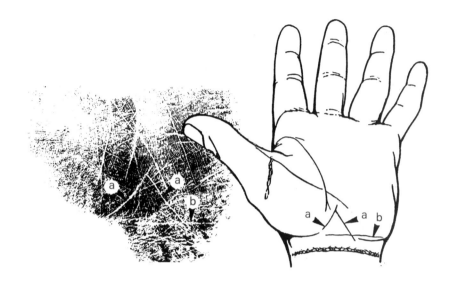

Women's troubles

Disturbances low down on the mount of Neptune indicate problems for women. If there is a triangle formation there that suddenly fills up with fine, broken bits of line or if the area suddenly becomes red, pregnancy is the reason!

A single wart represents a temporary problem. If the wart is on the palm, the person is his own worst enemy, but if it is on the back of the hand, someone else is causing the problem. Once again, relate this to the part of the hand or finger in question.

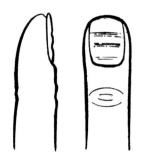

Fingernails take around six to eight months to grow out from root to tip, so they show current or recent health and emotional problems. Lateral dents show a period of illness or an upset when the nail was forming.

Longitudinal ridges suggest problems with bones and ligaments; the corresponding finger will show you the part of the body that is affected.

A shock to the system

♦ Jupiter fingernail—on or near the head

♦ Saturn fingernail—the shoulders, spine, ribs, or pelvis

♦ Apollo fingernail—the arms and legs

♦ Mercury fingernail—the forearms, wrists, lower legs, ankles, and feet

Old palmistry books talk of "Hippocratic nails" or "watchglass nails." If you imagine an old pocket watch—the kind

Arthritis and other problems in or around the bones

that used to hang on a chain—the glass on the front was usually a convex, or lens, shape. These nails revealed that the person was suffering from tuberculosis.

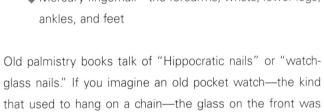

I never thought to see this in modern times, but some years ago, I was giving sample readings while promoting my books in a bookstore. A young woman sat down and gave me her hands. I always start by looking at the back of the hand, so the first thing I saw was a full set of watch-glass nails. This was a real first for me, and I commented that old palmistry texts would have said that she had TB. She told me that the old books were right, because she had recently been in the hospital for TB, which she had caught while traveling in India. She was no longer infectious and she was well on the way to recovery. I was very glad that day to remember the inoculation that we all had lined up for at school so many years before!

Watch-glass nails

I have also seen this in cases of lung cancer. Sometimes bunches of tiny, shiny warts appear on some area of the hands—especially on the sides of the hands—and this can be a warning of cancer or other tumors. Changes in the color or temperature of the hands can alert one to potential heart problems.

11

BACK TO THE BEGINNING

So now we return to the social scene that we set at the beginning of this book. Let us assume that you and your new pal have met and that you are getting to know each other. Let us also move on a little and see whether you can have a future together. For the sake of convenience, we will assume that you are female and that the object of your interest is male. However, everything in this chapter that relates to one gender can be said of the other one as well.

You may remember that we started by looking at hand size. If yours are small and the man's are large, he will appreciate the speed at which you move and the way that you get things done, but he will choose not to be rushed. He will appreciate quiet nights in, listening to records, and whiling away time. If his hands are small and yours are large, his enterprise and energy will amaze you, but you will find it hard to keep up with him. He gets bored very quickly, so take him ice-skating or bowling rather than expecting him to stay in night after night with videos and takeout as the only form of amusement.

Left- and right-handedness don't cause a problem, because the differences are complementary. One of you has a more artistic eye than the other, so the southpaw will help the right-hander to choose nice clothes and buy stylish things for the home. The right-hander will be happy with this unless his hands are extremely rigid.

If you have flexible hands and the object of your desire has stiff ones, don't expect him to drop everything and jump on an airplane with you—and don't ask him to accompany you on a minimalist backpacking vacation. He needs time to plan things, and he needs to take everything with him, including the kitchen sink. On the other hand, if he has flexible hands, you can expect him to ask you to take a trip up the Amazon with nothing but a tooth- brush and a spare pair of socks.

A "busy" hand that is full of lines means that the owner has a fussy and neurotic personality. If you are also a "busy-handed" worrier who picks up other people's anxieties and gets worked up quickly, a similar partner will understand where you are coming from. Someone with a clear hand has a quiet voice and manner, but he can erupt into sarcasm and temper or long bouts of sulky moodiness when things don't go his way. You have to work out for your- self which of these two evils is easiest to live with. A fine skin tone denotes sensitivity and refinement; a coarser one shows a more basic nature.

Flexible hands can travel light

It is important for a couple to have similar views about money, so look at the way his fingers spread. If they spread widely, with wide gaps where the fingers join the hands, you can expect him to be generous and to spend freely on nights out and on having fun. This might be great while you are dating, but don't expect him to become Mr. Responsibility overnight when you settle down.

A man whose fingers are tightly joined, so that light doesn't show through the gaps, will guard his finances closely. He might also be secretive. If you like a guy who has a good

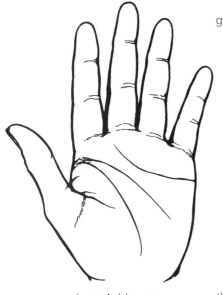

A sociable man

grip on his finances and who doesn't tell the world his business, this is the man for you—especially if his fingertips are squared off at the ends. He will give you great financial advice, but if you are looking for fun . . . well, you may not get much. For a reasonable attitude toward money, look for hands that are neither too spread out nor too "tightfisted." Also, look for a thumb that is reasonably flexible but not so double-jointed that the ball can turn right back.

A sociable man has rounded fingertips and a thumb that opens widely. He will try to get along with your friends and family, and he will be helpful, especially if his fingertips bend back when you press them.

If you prefer to live deep in the country with horses, farm animals, and nature, your hands will be square. You should choose a lover with similarly square hands.

Take the man's hand to assess whether he is a hard worker, because a firm hand belongs to a hard worker while a soft one tells you that he is self-indulgent and lazy. This is fine if he has an independent income, but this is not so good if he hopes that his girlfriend will take care of him. On the other hand, a guy who drives himself hard might have little time to spare, and you may find yourself waiting around at home while he is earning his next million dollars. If your hands are hard, you won't mind pulling your weight in the home or out

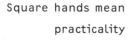

Square hands mean practicality

136

at work, but if they are soft, you definitely need a man to "take care of you" and to make decisions for you.

If your fingers are smooth, and especially if they are long and artistic, you may be impractical and allergic to dealing with details. In this case, look for a lover with knotty knuckles, because he loves detailed work.

So what about sex? There are few rules here, really, but a man with large hands will take his time over lovemaking and will be less inclined to kinkiness than a smaller-handed one. Also, look for a wide mount of Venus. The man with a high mount will want frequent sex; the one with a flatter Venus may be a great lover, but he will not need to make love as often. The height of the mount depends to some extent upon the hardness of the hand.

When the mount of Venus is cramped, there might be something unusual in his approach. A friend of mine dated a pleasant man who had a very narrow mount of Venus. The conversation was great (this man has an active mind), but the lovemaking was distinctly odd, because he liked it best when she dressed in strange "grandmotherly" underwear that he bought for her. At least his kink was not a danger to her or to anyone else, but it took the shine off the relationship!

Look at your own mount of Venus and your Mercury finger. If they show signs of sexiness (a well-formed Venus and a Mercury finger that is wider on the lower phalange than the two upper ones), then for goodness sake, choose a loving man. A man who prefers to spend his spare time making model airplanes or growing huge onions may suit someone (goodness knows who), but he won't suit you.

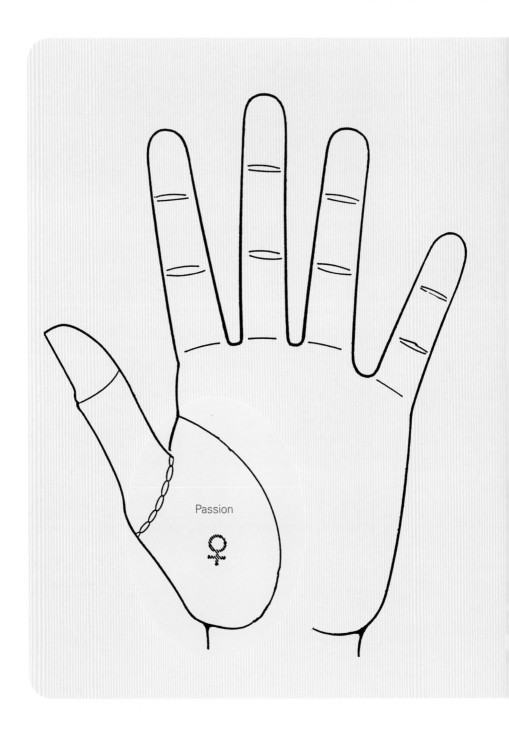

Passion

A very large and high mount of Venus shows a lust for life and for lovemaking. This guy will leave you trembling, and you will look back on the hours that you spent with him with great fondness. However, he won't resist leaving a few other women with good memories as well! Indeed, he may make spine-tingling love for hours and then forget all about you the moment he closes your door behind him as he leaves.

The life line can tell you something about his sexual approach. If it is deep and strong, he will want frequent sex, but he may not be the most imaginative or generous of lovers. A lighter, more feathered life line shows refinement and a generous attitude. If your own life line is vigorous, your sexual needs are strong, but if it is weak, you can only relax and respond when you feel cherished and loved. You will shrink inside yourself and protect yourself if your partner hurts or upsets you. If life outside your relationship makes you anxious, sad, or angry, or if someone bullies or harasses you, your sexual needs will temporarily switch off.

Now see whether you can sneak a look at his heart line. Let us also say that he is African American and gorgeous with the happiest smile, while you are Asian and equally lovely. If his heart line runs straight across both his hands, he will not want to introduce you to his mother or his friends. If it curves on his left hand, he won't care at all for anyone else's opinions about whom he dates. A curved heart line on both hands means that he will marry for love—and if he loves you, that is good enough for him. Naturally, your heart line is also important here. After all, you need to know in your heart whether you have a mental checklist to complete of social and cultural characteristics, or whether the fires of romance will be enough for you.

Choose a man with a nice clear head line, and at least you will know that he is sane. A few small branches on the line or even a small island are all right, because they show gains and losses in life, but a real mess on this line suggests that something is wrong with his health or his mentality. If your own head line is a mess, get some treatment.

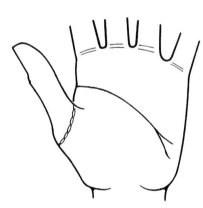

This man will send you flowers and poems

A smooth life line suggests a smooth path in life, with few changes. At least you know that what you see is what you get, and your life with this guy will run pretty much to plan. See if it curves around at the lower end or if it travels out into the palm. He will want to stay close to home if it curves. He may not be able to cut the apron strings if his life and head line are very tied and if the fate line starts from somewhere around the life line. If the life line travels outward, the man will focus on his work and will wish to travel. A line that forks shows an interest in many areas of life. See if your life line matches his. A little difference adds spice to a relationship, but a major one can make it a disaster.

If he is an older man with an attachment line that is close to the heart line, child lines, and a curved life line, don't believe him when he tells you that he has never been married. He may even still be so.

There are many more things to look out for, but here are some that are good to avoid. A thick, fat percussion edge that bows outward is a sign of violence. Stiff, small fingers that show little light and gestures that show you the backs of his hands rather than the palms show aggression and the need to "handle" others. This man can be verbally or physically aggressive. The same goes for large, thick, coarse-skinned hands.

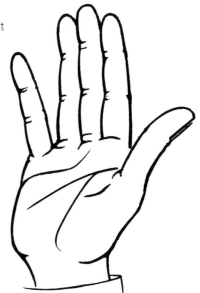

An untroubled life

A long Saturn finger might indicate an interest in religion—especially if the fingertip is pointy. A very short Saturn finger shows that this man is happiest when taking risks or even gambling.

Look to your own hands and see what you want out of life and love; then check to see if your new acquaintance is different . . . but not too different from you. Then you could really be in business!

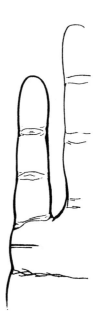

Can you trust this man?

12

HOW TO MAKE HANDPRINTS

A quick way to make a handprint is to cover the hand with dark lipstick and then place the hand onto some fine or flimsy paper, pressing the paper gently up into the center of the hand and then peeling it off. However, if you are going to do the job properly, you will need the right tools.

THE EQUIPMENT YOU WILL NEED

Paint or Ink

Go to an art shop and buy some water-based block-printing ink. This ink looks like a tube of paint or even toothpaste. Use black, dark red, or any other dark color rather than white.

Look for Block Printing Ink, which comes in many colors. Oil-based inks smear and are hard to wash off the hands and clothes. You can buy tiny tubes of fingerprint ink from art shops. This is much finer-grained than Block Printing Ink, but it is oil-based and difficult to use for whole hands.

A Roller

You need to buy a rubber-coated paste-up roller from an art shop. The roller should be about two inches wide and about one inch in diameter.

A Tile or Plate

A bathroom tile is fine if you have a spare one lying around, but if you don't, use an old china plate.

Paper Towels

This is the roll of paper towels that we all use for mopping up spills.

A Pen

A felt-tipped pen for drawing around the hand.

Paper

Any normal photocopy or inkjet paper is fine. Expensive papers do a worse job than inexpensive ones because they are often coated with a layer of fine clay.

Also . . .

Supply aprons for yourself and your guinea pig. Also have handy a basin or sink with plenty of soap, an old towel or cloth for washing the mess off afterward, and what else? Oh, yes, you need a guinea pig!

METHOD

1 Put several sheets of paper towel on top of each other to make a soft base. Take a couple more sheets and fold them in half in order to make a slight ridge or mound, and lay the ridge across the middle of your pile.

Use several sheets of paper towel

2 Lay several sheets of paper on top of the stack of
paper towels.

Use several sheets of paper

3 Squeeze a little of the ink onto your plate or tile—about half an inch will do.

Use just a small amount

4 Run the roller up and down in the ink until it is well covered but not too thickly or wetly covered.

Don't overink the roller

5 Now cover your friend's hand with ink. Do not lay the ink on too thickly or it will end up in an unreadable smudge.

This is the fun part

6 Ask your friend to relax his hand a little, and then place it on the paper with the palm located over the slight mound in the middle. Do not press down heavily on his hand or you will smudge the print. Just give the area where the fingers and thumb join the hand a light press.

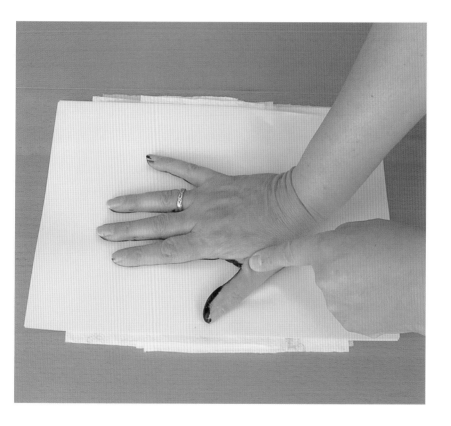

Do this slowly

7 Leave the hand in place for a moment or two, and then take the felt-tipped pen and draw around it. Don't angle the pen in around the fingers or you will spoil the shape. Just outline them. If you can't get between two fingers, don't push the pen in; just go around the tops.

Keep the pen upright here

8 Now hold the paper down at the top and bottom and ask your friend to lift his hand beginning with the wrist end, slowly, until it is free of the paper.

9 Now mark whether this was the left or right hand, write your friend's name and age, and date the print. Now do the same thing with your friend's other hand, and then leave the prints to dry completely. Once the print is dry, the best thing to do is to photocopy it and put the original into one of those plastic pockets that fit into a ring binder.

If the hand is hollow in the middle, you will end up with a gap in the middle of the print. In this case, take another print, going as far as outlining the hand with the felt-tipped pen. Then ask your friend to carefully lift his hand up a little at the wrist end, with the paper still stuck to it; slowly and gently insert your hand under the sheet of paper, and gently press your fingers into the middle of his hand. Comment to him that money comes to those who have a slight hollow in their hands—although they usually have to earn it the hard way!

If you still cannot get a reasonable print of the center of the hand, rest the bottom of a piece of paper on a rolling pin or a wine bottle and put the heel of your friend's hand on top. Roll the pin forward and allow the hand to rest on the paper as it rolls along. This will distort the finger shapes, but it will give you a print of the middle of the hand. In this case, clip the two types of print together so that you have all the information that you need for your files or for future reference. If you make a print of your own hands, take another print every few months to see whether there have been any changes, however small.

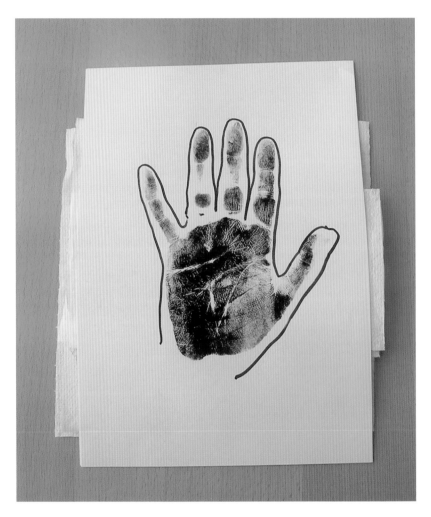

The finished hand print

DON'T PHOTOCOPY HANDS

Some people try to photocopy hands, but this doesn't give a readable copy. In the days when I gave consultations for a living, I occasionally received photocopied prints through the mail. These were hopeless, and I never understood how the sender could imagine that I would be able to read anything from these images.

A FEW FINAL TIPS

It is always worth writing the date on a handprint, so that you can spot any changes which may occur year to year.

Here is a tip for those occasions when you do not want to take a print but you are having a hard time seeing the small lines clearly. Rub a small amount of talcum powder onto the hard-to-read areas, such as child lines. You will be able to see them clearly!

If you do readings at a fund-raising event, be sure to bring a good table lamp and extension cord with you, as good lighting is very important.

Never try to shock people with traumatic news. If you see something nasty on a hand, sweeten the pill and minimize the news. It may not actually be too important, since hands can sometimes make a minor topic look more serious than it really is.

Being able to read hands can make you very popular, but it can also become a nuisance if people pester you for readings when you are out socially and are not in the mood to read hands. Some people can be selfish and become extremely persistent. If so, make an appointment at a more appopriate time and place—and at a convenient location! Reading for strangers is excellent practice and will help expand your knowledge and skill.

One final point: if you are a woman, do not invite men to your home or any other private location—no matter how much they insist. Go to a cafe or other public area to do the reading. Unfortunately, others may see you, and you will soon find yourself reading hands the rest of the day!

INDEX

Allergy line (via lasciva), 103
Angle of dexterity, 39
Angle of harmony, 39
Apollo
    finger, 44–45, 47
    indicators of, 28, 32
    line, 94, 95–97
    mount of, 32
Arch fingerprints, 51
Astrology. See Planets; specific planets
Attachment lines, 106–108
Busy hands, 135
Child lines, 112–113
Cold hands, 127
Color of hands, 127, 128
Composite fingerprints, 52
Countryside loop, 123
Coup de foudre, 115
Crosses, 119
Diamonds, 120
Discoloration, 128
Dots, 97–98, 120, 128
Elementary hands, 12–13
Family line, 100–101
Fate line, 83–91
    direction of, 86
    end of, 91
    events on, 88–89
    general indicators, 83–85
    lines joining, 87–88
    moving, 89–90
    start of, 85–86
    timing on, 87
Finances. See Money
Fingernails, 50–51, 130–131
Fingerprints, 51–53, 121–122
Fingers, 41–53. See also Phalanges
    Apollo, 44–45, 47
    illustrated, 43
    inclination of, 44–45

Jupiter, 44, 46
    long/short, 45
    Mercury, 45, 47–48, 137
    relaxed, 45
    Saturn, 44–45, 46–47, 141
    settings of, 43–44
    thumb and, 24–25, 58–61
    tightly curled, 45
Fingertips, 48–50
    shape of, 48–49
    thickness of, 50
Flexibility, of hands, 57, 134–135
Gay or straight, 81
Girdle of Venus, 101
Grilles, 120, 128
Hand, map of, 27–39. See also Mounts
    angles, 39
    illustrated, 29, 30
    planets and, 28
Handprints, making, 143–156
    equipment needed, 144–145
    method for, 146–154
Hand size
    large hands, 13–16, 21, 134
    less developed hands, 12–13
    of men, 10–16, 134
    small hands, 10–13, 134
Hand types
    elementary, 12–13
    knotty, knobby, 14–15
    large, 13–16, 21
    long, delicate, 14
    men, 10–16
    rounded, 11
    small, 10–13, 21
    square, 13
    thick "percussion", 15,

141
women, 21–22
Head line, 70–77
   general indicators,
   70–72
   health indicators, 128
   relationships and, 140
   start of, 72
   straight/curved/sloping,
   73–74
   variations on, 74–75
Healers, 33
Health indicators, 125–131
   color of hands, 127, 128
   fingernails, 130–131
   general appearance,
   126–127
   lines, 128–129
Health lines, 97–98
Heart line, 76, 77–81
   curved/straight, 78–79
   disturbed, 80
   in friendships, 80
   gay or straight, 81
   general indicators,
   77–78
   health indicators, 128
   health on, 81
   long/short, 78
   male/female relation-
   ships and, 77–80,
   139–140
   mystic cross, 80–81
   start of, 78
Hot hands, 127
Interference lines, 114–115
Islands
   under Apollo, 75
   on child lines, 113
   on fate line, 88–89
   under Jupiter, 128
   under Saturn, 75, 128
   on travel line, 100
Jupiter
   finger, 44, 46
   indicators of, 28, 31
   island under, 128
   mount of, 31, 118
Large hands, 13–16, 21,

134
Left-handedness, 16–17,
134
Life line, 64, 65–70
   end of, 70
   forked lines, 66–67
   general indicators,
   65–66
   health indicators, 128
   marks on, 68–69
   relationships and, 139,
   140–141
   rising lines, 69
   sexual approach and,
   139
   shadow lines, 69–70
   starting point, 68
   traveling line, 66
Lines. See Major lines;
Minor lines; specific lines
Loop fingerprints, 52
Loop skin ridges, 122–123
Love and relationships,
104–115, 134–141. See also
Men, evaluating; Women,
evaluating
   attachment lines,
   106–108
   busy hands, 135
   child lines, 112–113
   death of partner, 108
   easy/challenging rela-
   tionships, 109–112
   flexible/inflexible hands
   and, 57, 134–135
   general indicators,
   106–108
   head line and, 140
   heart line and, 77–80,
   139–140
   interference lines,
   114–115
   life line and, 139,
   140–141
   money and, 24–25,
   135–136
   passionate affairs, 115
   sexual interests/skills,
   12, 23–24, 137–139

sibling lines, 114
Luna
    fate line and, 85
    indicators of, 28, 35–36
    mount of, 23–24, 35–36
Major lines, 63–91
    fate line. *See* Fate line
    head line, 70–77, 128,
    140
    heart line, 76, 77–81,
    128, 139–140
    life line, 64, 65–70, 128,
    139
    semi-simian line, 82
    simian line, 82
Marks, 117–123
    crosses, 119
    minor, 120
    skin ridge patterns,
    121–123
    squares, 118–119
    stars, 119
Mars
    indicators of, 28, 37–38
    lower, 38
    mount of, 37–38
    upper, 37–38
Memory loop, 123
Men, evaluating, 9–17. *See
also* Love and relation-
ships
    elementary hands,
    12–13
    hand size, 10–16, 134
    right- or left-handed-
    ness, 16–17, 134
    rounded hands, 11
    sexual interests/skills,
    12, 137–139
    work ethic, 136–137
Mercury
    finger, 45, 47–48, 137
    indicators of, 28, 33
    mount of, 33, 128
Military lines, 102
Minor lines, 93–103
    Apollo line, 94, 95–97
    family line, 100–101
    girdle of Venus, 101

military lines, 102
    moneymaker line, 102
    rascettes, 103
    ring of Solomon, 102
    travel lines, 98–100
    via lasciva (allergy line),
    103
Money
    relationships and,
    135–136
    shopping and, 24–25
Moneymaker line, 102
Moon. *See* Luna
Mount of Venus, 23
Mounts
    of Apollo, 32
    illustrated, 29, 30
    of Jupiter, 31, 118
    of Luna, 35–36
    of Mars, 37–38
    of Mercury, 33, 128
    of Neptune, 39, 129
    of Pluto, 36
    of Saturn, 32
    of Venus, 34–35, 36,
    137–139
Mystic cross, 80–81
Neptune
    fate line and, 83, 85
    indicators of, 28, 39
    mount of, 39, 129
Passion. *See also* Love
and relationships
    intense love affairs, 115
    Luna mount and, 23–24
    seat of, 23, 34–35
    sexual interests/skills,
    12, 23–24, 137–139
    Venus mount and, 23,
    34–35
Peacock's eye fingerprints,
52
Phalanges, 55–61. *See
also* Fingers
    defined, 56
    first, short, 24
    flexible/inflexible, 57,
    134–135
    general indicators, 56

spacing of, 57
thumb, 24–25, 58–61
turning upward, 57
vertical creases, 56–57
Photocopying hands, 155
Pits, 120, 128
Planets. *See also specific planets*
astrology, palmistry and, 28
characteristics of, 28
chart of, 28
mounts of. *See* Mounts
Pluto
indicators of, 28, 36
mount of, 36
Pointed fingertips, 49
Rajah loop, 122
Rascettes, 103
Readings, giving, 155–156
Relationships. *See* Love and relationships; Men, evaluating; Women, evaluating
Right-handedness, 16–17, 134
Ring of Solomon, 102
Rounded fingertips, 49
Saturn
fate line and, 83
finger, 44–45, 46–47, 141
indicators of, 28, 32
island under, 75, 128
mount of, 32
Saturn line. *See* Fate line
Semi-simian line, 82
Sex. *See* Passion
Sexual orientation, 81
Shopping, 24–25
Sibling lines, 114
Simian line, 82
Skin ridge patterns, 121–123
Small hands, 10–13, 134
Softness, of hands, 126
Spatulate fingertips, 49
Squares, 118–119
Stars, 119

Stray lines, 120
Tasseled lines, 120
Tented arch fingerprints, 52
Thumbs, 58–61
bent backward vs. straight, 24–25
lower phalange, 61
setting/inclination, 58–59
top phalange, 60–61
Travel. *See* Luna
Travel lines, 66, 98–100
Triangles, 120
Tri-radius mark, 123
Uranus, 28
Venus
girdle of, 101
indicators of, 28, 34–35
mount of, 34–35, 36, 137–139
Via lasciva (allergy line), 103
Warts, 129
Whorl fingerprints, 52
Women, evaluating, 19–25. *See also* Love and relationships
brain power, 24
first phalanges and, 24
hand shape, 22
large vs. small hands, 21
money/shopping, 24–25
needs, desires, willfulness, 21–22
radial side of hand, 22
sexual interests/skills, 23–24, 137–139
ulna side of hand, 21